AF352197

Sidney Hook

A Checklist of Writings

Compiled by
Barbara Levine

Southern Illinois University Press

Carbondale and Edwardsville

Library of Congress Cataloging-in-Publication Data

Levine, Barbara, 1937-
Sidney Hook: a checklist of writings / compiled by Barbara Levine.
    p.   cm.
Includes indexes.
1. Hook, Sidney, 1902-   --Bibliography.   I. Title.
Z8414.938.L48 1988
[B945.H684]
016.191--dc19
ISBN 0-8093-1510-6   88-15043
                                                      CIP

Contents

Preface

In a 1926 recommendation to the Department of Philosophy, Columbia University, John Dewey wrote about Sidney Hook:

> He combines originality with orderly method in both study and statement. His range of information in the history of thought . . . was as broad, accurate, digested and lucidly expressed as that of any student I have ever examined. I regard him as one of the most promising students in philosophy I have had to do with in my forty years of teaching.

One year later Dewey wrote to George Herbert Mead, "He has a section in his dissertation on the metaphysics of the instrument which is a corker. I almost feel that I am ready to quit, as he has not only got the point but sees many implications I hadn't seen."

In the writings listed here, Hook has, since the mid-1920s, shown clearly that Dewey's assessment of his ability was warranted. He has amply fulfilled Dewey's expectations; he continues to do so in 1988 at a brisk clip. Sidney Hook has authored or edited over forty books; these books have been extensively reviewed, as evidenced by the thirty-eight located reviews of his 1987 autobiography, *Out of Step*. Attesting to his interest in varied topics, Hook has been a prolific reviewer himself, publishing at least 250 reviews since 1928 (including two already in 1988). In addition, he has written numerous forewords, introductions, and prefaces to books covering a wide range of subjects.

This checklist of writings by Sidney Hook lists his located published writings from 1922 to the present, a period of sixty-six years. These items appeared in publications as diverse as *New Masses* and *National Review*, *Time* and *Journal of Philosophy*, *Sunday Australian* and *Brattleboro* (Vt.) *Reformer*, and *Christian Register* and *Contemporary Jewish Record*. The range of these publications indicates the breadth and depth of his interests.

The checklist lists books, parts of books, articles, reviews, and published letters arranged chronologically by date of first publication. When articles have been reprinted in a Hook collection or edition, that reprinting is listed under the first publication; other reprintings are omitted. Reviews of Hook's major works appear under the work reviewed.

The checklist is intended to be exhaustive. It includes replies to Hook's writing and comments to which he has responded, all of which are

listed under the first Hook publication to which they refer. All items
have been verified and, when possible, copies obtained. These items are
now collected at the Center for Dewey Studies, Southern Illinois University
at Carbondale.

A title-subject index serves as a guide to facilitate location of specific
Hook items. Works reviewed by Hook are indexed alphabetically by author
under Reviews. Forewords, Introductions, and Prefaces follow the same
pattern. Untitled letters are indexed alphabetically by periodical under Letters. A name index (including those with whom Hook interacted along with
authors of books he has reviewed) is supplied for the reader's convenience.

This checklist has been compiled by the staff of the Center for Dewey
Studies under the direction of Barbara Levine, textual editor, assisted by
Richard Field, who did much of the library research; Diane Meierkort, who
began typing the text; and Anne Sharpe, textual editor, who completed the
word processing, prepared the indexes, and assisted in the editing.

We are indebted to John Dennis Crowley, S.J., for his work on the
"Bibliography of Sidney Hook," in *Sidney Hook and the Contemporary
World*, ed. Paul Kurtz (New York: John Day Co., 1968), pp. 429-71. An ear-
lier, necessarily incomplete, Dewey Center checklist compiled by Jo Ann
Boydston and Kathleen Poulos appeared in *Sidney Hook: Philosopher of
Democracy and Humanism*, ed. Paul Kurtz (Buffalo, N.Y.: Prometheus
Books, 1983), pp. 311-55.

We acknowledge with gratitude the assistance given us by Dale Reed,
Assistant Archivist, Hoover Institution on War, Revolution and Peace,
Stanford University.

B. L.
May, 1988

Checklist

1922

"The Philosophy of Non-Resistance." *Open Court* 36 (Jan. 1922): 1-5.

"A Philosophical Dialogue." *Open Court* 36 (Oct. 1922): 621-26.

1926

Review of **The Logical Influence of Hegel on Marx,** by Rebecca Cooper. *Journal of Philosophy* 23 (18 Feb. 1926): 106-8.

"The Metaphysics of *Leading Principles*." *Journal of Philosophy* 23 (1 Apr. 1926): 169-83.
[Reprinted in **The Metaphysics of Pragmatism,** 1927.]

"Methodological Considerations in Primitive Art." *Open Court* 40 (June 1926): 328-39.

1927

The Metaphysics of Pragmatism. Chicago: Open Court Publishing Co., 1927.
[Reviewed in *Dial* 85 (Oct. 1928): 360; *Journal of Philosophy* 25 (21 June 1928): 356-59 (Scott Buchanan); *London Mercury* 18 (Oct. 1928): 666-69 (J. J. Stocks); *Mind* 37 (Apr. 1928): 242-43 (F. C. S. Schiller).]

Collected Works of Vladimir Ilyich Lenin, translated by Sidney Hook and David Kvitko. New York: International Publishers, 1927.

"The Ethics of Suicide." *International Journal of Ethics* 37 (Jan. 1927): 173-88.

"Freedom." *Open Court* 41 (Feb. 1927): 65-73.
[Reprinted in **The Metaphysics of Pragmatism,** 1927.]

"Categorial Analysis and Pragmatic-Realism." *Journal of Philosophy* 24 (31

Mar. 1927): 169-87.
[Reprinted in **The Metaphysics of Pragmatism**, 1927.]

"The Metaphysics of the Instrument, Part 1." *Monist* 37 (July 1927): 335-
56. "Part 2: Thinking as Instrumental." Ibid. 37 (Oct. 1927): 601-19.
"Part 3: The Ethics of the Instrument." Ibid., 620-23.
[Reprinted in **The Metaphysics of Pragmatism**, 1927.]

"The Irrationality of *the Irrational*." *Journal of Philosophy* 24 (4 Aug. 1927):
421-37.

1928

"Marx and Freud: Oil and Water." *Open Court* 41 (Jan. 1928): 20-25.
Comment on Max Eastman, "Karl Marx Anticipated Freud." *New
Masses* 3 (July 1927): 11-12.

"The Philosophy of Dialectical Materialism, Parts 1 and 2." Review of
Materialism and Empirio-Criticism, by Vladimir I. Lenin. *Journal of
Philosophy* 25 (1 Mar. 1928): 113-24; ibid. 25 (15 Mar. 1928): 141-55.
Reply by Max Eastman, ibid. 25 (16 Aug. 1928): 475-76.
Rejoinder by Hook, ibid. 25 (11 Oct. 1928): 587-88.

"Marxism, Metaphysics, and Modern Science." Review of **Marx, Lenin, and
the Science of Revolution**, by Max Eastman. *Modern Quarterly* 4 (May-
Aug. 1928): 388-94.
For the debate that ensued, see:
Eastman, "As to Sidney Hook's Morals." Ibid. 5 (Nov. 1928-Feb.
1929): 85-87.
Hook, "As to Max Eastman's Mentality." Ibid., 88-91.
Eastman, "Excommunication *and* Exorcism *as* Critical Methods, Part
1." *Modern Monthly* 7 (May 1933): 210-13.
Hook, review of **Karl Marx's "Capital" and Other Writings**, by Max
Eastman. Ibid., 248-50.
Eastman, "A Master Magician, Part 2." Ibid. 7 (June 1933): 290-93,
307.
Eastman, letter in reply to Hook's review of **Karl Marx's "Capital"
and Other Writings**. Ibid., 320.
Eastman, "Man and History." Ibid. 7 (July 1933): 348-50.
Hook, "A Note from Sidney Hook." Ibid., 350-51.
Eastman, letter in reply. Ibid. 7 (Aug. 1933): 447-48.
Hook, letter to the editor. Ibid., 510-11.
V. F. Calverton, "To Max Eastman and Sidney Hook." Ibid., 511-12.
Eastman, letter. Ibid. 7 (Oct. 1933): 576.

"Freedom." *Archiv für systematische Philosophie und Soziologie* 31 (1928):
17-26. [Concluding chapter of **The Metaphysics of Pragmatism,**
1927.]

1929

"What Is Dialectic? I." *Journal of Philosophy* 26 (14 Feb. 1929): 85-99. "II."
Ibid. 26 (28 Feb. 1929): 113-23.

Review of **Hegels Staatsidee,** by Julius Löwenstein. *Journal of Philosophy*
26 (12 Sept. 1929): 526-30.

"A Pragmatic Critique of the Historico-Genetic Method." In **Essays in
Honor of John Dewey, on the Occasion of His Seventieth Birthday,** 156-
74. New York: Henry Holt and Co., 1929.

1930

"A Critique of Ethical Realism." *International Journal of Ethics* 40 (Jan.
1930): 179-210.
[Reprinted, with slight changes, in **Pragmatism and the Tragic Sense of
Life,** 1974.]

"A Personal Impression of Contemporary German Philosophy." *Journal of
Philosophy* 27 (13 Mar. 1930): 141-60.
Reply by Dorion Cairns, "Mr. Hook's Impression of Phenomenol-
ogy." Ibid. 27 (17 July 1930): 393-96.
Rejoinder by Hook, "In Defence of an Impression." Ibid. 27 (6 Nov.
1930): 635-37.

"The Revolt Against Dualism." Review of **The Revolt Against Dualism,** by
Arthur O. Lovejoy. *New Republic* 63 (18 June 1930): 129-30.

"Husserl's Phenomenological Idealism." Review of **Formale und Trans-
zendentale Logik,** by Edmund Husserl. *Journal of Philosophy* 27 (3 July
1930): 365-80.

"Contemporary American Philosophy." Review of **Contemporary
American Philosophy: Personal Statements,** edited by George P. Adams
and William P. Montague. *New Republic* 63 (16 July 1930): 237-39.

"The Philosophy of Morris R. Cohen." *New Republic* 63 (23 July 1930):
278-81.

4

"Capitalism and Protestantism." Review of **The Protestant Ethic and the Spirit of Capitalism**, by Max Weber. *Nation* 131 (29 Oct. 1930): 476-78.

Review of **The American Road to Culture**, by George S. Counts. *Current History* 33 (Oct. 1930): x-xiii.

"The Meaning of Marxism." Part of a symposium on "Marxism and Social Change." *Modern Quarterly* 5 (Winter 1930-31): 430-35.
   Comment in *Revolutionary Age*, 7 Feb. 1931, 4.

"The Non-Sense of *the* Whole." Review of **The Re-discovery of America: An Introduction to a Philosophy of American Life**, by Waldo Frank. *Modern Quarterly* 5 (Winter 1930-31): 504-13.
   Reply by Frank, ibid., 514-16.

Encyclopaedia of the Social Sciences, edited by Edwin R. A. Seligman. New York: Macmillan Co., 1930-35.
   Contributions:
       "Bauer, Bruno." Vol. 2, 1930, 481.
       "Büchner, Ludwig." Vol. 3, 1931, 30.
       "Determinism." Vol. 5, 1931, 110-14.
       "Dietzgen, Joseph." Vol. 5, 1931, 139.
       "Engels, Friedrich." Vol. 5, 1931, 540-41.
       "Feuerbach, Ludwig Andreas." Vol. 6, 1931, 221-22.
       "Materialism." Vol. 10, 1933, 209-20.
       "Ruge, Arnold." Vol. 13, 1934, 462-63.
       "Violence." Vol. 15, 1935, 264-67.

1931

Review of **The Psychology of Socialism**, by Henri DeMan. *Current History* 33 (Jan. 1931): xxi-xxiii.

"The New Individualism." Review of **Individualism Old and New**, by John Dewey. *Current History* 33 (Mar. 1931): xxii-xxiv.

"The Soviet Challenge." Review of **The Soviet Challenge to America**, by George S. Counts. *Current History* 34 (May 1931): xiii-xiv.

"John Dewey and His Critics." *New Republic* 67 (3 June 1931): 73-74.

"Marx and Darwinism." *New Republic* 67 (29 July 1931): 290.
   See Robert Morss Lovett's review of **America's Way Out**, by Norman Thomas. Ibid. 67 (20 May 1931): 22-23.
       Reply by Lovett, ibid. 67 (29 July 1931): 290-91.

"Towards the Understanding of Karl Marx." *Symposium* 2 (July 1931): 325-67.
[Reprinted in **Towards the Understanding of Karl Marx**, 1933.]

Review of **Hegel und die Hegelsche Schule,** by Willy Moog. *Journal of Philosophy* 28 (27 Aug. 1931): 497-500.

"Experimental Logic." *Mind* 40 (Oct. 1931): 424-38.

Review of **Ideas--General Introduction to Pure Phenomenology,** by Edmund Husserl. *Symposium* 2 (Oct. 1931): 531-40.

"The Metaphysics of Experience." Review of **Philosophy and Civilization,** by John Dewey. *New Republic* 68 (4 Nov. 1931): 330-31.

"From Hegel to Marx." *Modern Quarterly* 6 (Winter 1931): 46-62; ibid. 6 (Summer 1932): 33-43; ibid. 6 (Autumn 1932): 58-67.
[Reprinted in **From Hegel to Marx**, 1936.]

1932

"Reason and Nature: The Metaphysics of Scientific Method." Review of **Reason and Nature,** by Morris R. Cohen. *Journal of Philosophy* 29 (7 Jan. 1932): 5-24.

Review of **Hegel: Sein Wollen und Sein Werk,** vol. 1, by Theodor L. Haering. *Philosophical Review* 41 (Jan. 1932): 75-77.

"An Epic of Revolution." Review of **The Overthrow of Tzarism. The History of the Russian Revolution,** vol. 1, by Leon Trotsky. *Saturday Review* 8 (27 Feb. 1932): 549-51.

"Pictures of the Past." Review of **History of Russia,** vol. 1, by M. N. Pokrovsky. *Saturday Review* 8 (30 Apr. 1932): 700.

Review of **Human Values,** by DeWitt H. Parker. *International Journal of Ethics* 42 (Apr. 1932): 348-53.

Review of **Principles of Philosophy. Collected Papers of Charles Sanders Peirce,** edited by Charles Hartshorne and Paul Weiss, vol. 1. *Symposium* 3 (Apr. 1932): 248-56.

Review of **Principles of Philosophy. Collected Papers of Charles Sanders Peirce,** edited by Charles Hartshorne and Paul Weiss, vol. 1. *Current History* 36 (May 1932): iv-v.

"The Contemporary Significance of Hegel's Philosophy. *Philosophical Review* 41 (May 1932): 237-60.

"Half-baked Communism." Review of **Breakdown: The Collapse of Traditional Civilisation**, by Robert Briffault. *Nation* 134 (8 June 1932): 654-55.
 Replies by M. F. Ashley-Montagu, Nelson Morris, and Briffault, ibid. 135 (13 July 1932): 36-37.
 Rejoinder by Hook, ibid. 135 (24 Aug. 1932): 170-71.

Review of **Hegel's Phenomenology of Mind**, 2d ed., translated by J. B. Baillie. *Journal of Philosophy* 29 (23 June 1932): 361-62.

"Myth, Fact, and Poetry of Soviet Russia." Review of **Bolshevism: Theory and Practice**, by Waldemar Gurian; **The Soviet Worker**, by Joseph Freeman; **Dawn in Russia**, by Waldo Frank; **Bolshevism, Fascism, and Capitalism**, by George S. Counts, Luigi Villari, Malcolm C. Rorty, and Newton D. Baker. *Nation* 135 (14 Sept. 1932): 237-38.

Review of **What Is to Be Done?** by Vladimir I. Lenin. *American Journal of Sociology* 38 (Sept. 1932): 315-17.

1933

Towards the Understanding of Karl Marx: A Revolutionary Interpretation. New York: John Day Co., 1933.
[Reviewed in *American Economic Review* 23 (Dec. 1933): 687-89 (Joseph J. Senturia); *American Political Science Review* 27 (Aug. 1933): 657-58 (Selig Perlman); *Boston Evening Transcript*, 12 Apr. 1933, 2; *City College Alumnus* 29 (May 1933): 71-72 (David P. Berenberg); *Commonweal* 18 (18 Aug. 1933): 390-91 (Ross J. S. Hoffman); *Current History* 38 (Aug. 1933): vi; *Journal of Philosophy* 30 (9 Nov. 1933): 634-37 (George H. Sabine); *Modern Monthly* 7 (Oct. 1933): 571-73 (Harry Slochower); *Nation* 136 (12 Apr. 1933): 414-15 (Benjamin Stolberg); *New Humanist* 6 (July-Aug. 1933): 38-40 (Llewellyn Jones); *New Republic* 75 (28 June 1933): 186-87 (Harold J. Laski); ibid. 91 (4 Aug. 1937): 366-68 (Edmund Wilson); *New York Herald Tribune Books*, 16 Apr. 1933, 6 (Max Eastman); *North American Review* 236 (July 1933): 96 (Herschel Brickell); *Philosophical Review* 44 (Jan. 1935): 73-75 (George E. G. Catlin); *Progressive Education* 10 (Oct. 1933): 354-55 (Lewis Carliner); *Saturday Review* 9 (22 Apr. 1933): 550 (Felix Morrow); *Student Outlook* 3 (Nov.-Dec. 1934): 31-34 (Morris R. Cohen); *Workers Age* 2 (1 Oct. 1933): 4, 8 (Jim Cork); *World Tomorrow* 16 (Aug. 1933): 476 (Reinhold Niebuhr).]

"Karl Marx and the Young Hegelians." *Modern Monthly* 7 (Feb. 1933): 33-44.

"Marxism--Dogma or Method?" *Nation* 136 (15 Mar. 1933): 284-85.
Reply by Leon Trotsky, ibid. 137 (5 July 1933): 18.
Response by Hook, ibid., 18-19.

"The Marxian Dialectic." *New Republic* 74 (22 Mar. 1933): 150-54.

"Russia in Solution." Review of **The History of the Russian Revolution,** vols. 2 and 3, by Leon Trotsky, translated by Max Eastman. *Saturday Review* 9 (8 Apr. 1933): 521-22.

Review of **Der Möglichkeitsgedanke Systemgeschichtliche Untersuchungen,** by August Faust. *Journal of Philosophy* 30 (13 Apr. 1933): 221-23.

"Against the Fascist Terror in Germany." *New Masses* 9 (Apr. 1933): 11-12.

"Karl Marx and Bruno Bauer." *Modern Monthly* 7 (Apr. 1933): 160-74.
[Reprinted in **From Hegel to Marx,** 1936.]

"Education and Politics." Review of **The Educational Frontier,** edited by William Heard Kilpatrick. *New Republic* 75 (24 May 1933): 49-50.

"Why the German Student Is Fascist." *Student Outlook* 1 (May 1933): 4-6, 20.

"Science and the Crisis." Review of **The Universe of Science,** by H. L. Levy, and **Science and the Changing World,** edited by Mary Adams. *Nation* 136 (21 June 1933): 705-6.

"Revolutionist's Symposium." Review of **Recovery through Revolution,** edited by Samuel D. Schmalhausen. *Nation* 136 (28 June 1933): 733-34.

"Kant and Political Liberalism," by Karl Marx, translated by Sidney Hook. *Modern Monthly* 7 (July 1933): 352-54.

"Arnold Ruge and Karl Marx, Part 1." *Modern Monthly* 7 (Aug. 1933): 409-21, 431; "Part 2." Ibid. 7 (Sept. 1933): 480-86.
[Reprinted in **From Hegel to Marx,** 1936.]

"De Libris--Disputatio." *City College Alumnus* 29 (Sept. 1933): 114-15.

"On Hegel's 'Concrete Universal,'" by Karl Marx, translated by Sidney Hook. *Modern Monthly* 7 (Sept. 1933): 496-97, 501.

"Karl Marx and Max Stirner." *Modern Monthly* 7 (Oct. 1933): 547-55, 569.
[Reprinted in **From Hegel to Marx**, 1936.]

"Psychology: The Social Bias." Review of **Seven Psychologies**, by Edna
Heidbreder. *New Republic* 77 (29 Nov. 1933): 81-82.

"Social Psychology--Marxian Style." Review of **Towards a United Front: A
Philosophy for American Workers**, by Leon Samson. *Modern Monthly* 7
(Nov. 1933): 637-39.

"Theories of Social Determinism." *Scientia* 54 (Dec. 1933): 437-49.

1934

The Democratic and Dictatorial Aspects of Communism. Part 2.
Worcester, Mass.: Carnegie Endowment for International Peace, 1934.
[Part 1: Joseph Stalin, **The Political and Social Doctrine of Com-
munism.**]

The Meaning of Marx, edited by Sidney Hook. Symposium by Bertrand
Russell, John Dewey, Morris R. Cohen, Sherwood Eddy, and Sidney
Hook. New York: Farrar and Rinehart, 1934.
[Reviewed in *Journal of Political Economy* 44 (Feb. 1936): 113-14 (M. M.
Bober); *Labour Monthly* 17 (Mar.-May 1935): 177-84, 249-56, 312-20 (L.
Rudas); *New Republic* 91 (4 Aug. 1937): 366-68 (Edmund Wilson);
Saturday Review 11 (2 Mar. 1935): 522 (Fabian Franklin).]

"The Meaning of Marx." In **The Meaning of Marx**, edited by Sidney Hook,
47-82. New York: Farrar and Rinehart, 1934.

"Is Marxism Compatible with Christianity?" *Christian Register* 113 (15 Feb.
1934): 103-6.
   Reply to Francis A. Henson, "The Challenge of Marxism to Christi-
      anity." Ibid. 113 (18 Jan. 1934): 35-38.
   Reply to Henry P. Van Dusen, "The Challenge of Christianity to
      Marxism." Ibid. 113 (1 Feb. 1934): 71-73.

"A Shot in the Dark." Review of **Lenin: A Biography**, by Ralph Fox. *Saturday Review* 10 (24 Feb. 1934): 503.

"The Philosophy of Technics in the U.S.S.R." *Modern Monthly* 8 (Feb.
1934): 31-36.

"The Nature of Discourse." Review of **Science and Sanity: An Introduction to Non-Aristotelian Systems and General Semantics**, by Alfred

Korzybski. *Saturday Review* 10 (10 Mar. 1934): 546-47.

"Dewey on Thought and Action." Review of **How We Think,** by John Dewey. *New Republic* 78 (21 Mar. 1934): 165.

"The Mythology of Class Science." *Modern Monthly* 8 (Mar. 1934): 112-17.

"What Is Materialism?" *Journal of Philosophy* 31 (26 Apr. 1934): 235-42.
     Reply by Roy W. Sellars, "Is Naturalism Enough?" Ibid. 41 (28 Sept. 1944): 533-44.
     Rejoinder by Hook, "Is Physical Realism Sufficient?" Ibid., 544-51.
[Reprinted in **The Meaning of Marx,** 1934.]

"A Symposium on Communism: Why I Am a Communist (Communism Without Dogmas)." *Modern Monthly* 8 (Apr. 1934): 143-65.
Bertrand Russell, "Why I Am Not a Communist." Ibid., 133-34.
John Dewey, "Why I Am Not a Communist." Ibid., 135-37.
Morris R. Cohen, "Why I Am Not a Communist." Ibid., 138-42.
     Comments by R. H. P., ibid. 8 (June 1934): 319-20.
     Letter by Hook, ibid., 320.
[Reprinted in **The Meaning of Marx,** 1934.]

"Marxism and Democracy: Some Notes on the Draft Program of the A.W.P." *Labor Action*, 1 May 1934, 5.

"The Role of the Educator." *Student Outlook* 2 (May 1934): 5-7.

"Sidney Hook Replies." *Commonwealth College Fortnightly* 10 (15 June 1934): 2-3.
     Reply to William Cunningham, "Misunderstanding Marxian Economics." Ibid. 10 (15 Feb. 1934): 2-3.
     Response by Paul Evans, "On Sydney [*sic*] Hook's Reply." Ibid. 10 (15 July 1934): 2-3.

"Socialism at the Crossroads." Review of **Socialism, Fascism and Communism,** edited by Joseph Shaplen and David Shub. *Saturday Review* 11 (21 July 1934): 1-2.

"The Fallacy of the Theory of Social Fascism." *Modern Monthly* 8 (July 1934): 342-52.

"The Challenge of the Social Order to the Curriculum of the Liberal Arts College." **In Report of the 11th Annual Meeting of the Fellows of the National Council on Religion in Higher Education,** Colgate-Rochester Divinity School, Rochester, N.Y., 4-10 Sept. 1934.

"An Open Letter to Lincoln Steffens." *Modern Monthly* 8 (Sept. 1934): 486-92.

Review of **Systematic Sociology on the Basis of the Beziehungslehre and Gebildelehre of Leopold Von Wiese**, adapted by Howard Becker. *Philosophical Review* 43 (Sept. 1934): 532-35.

Review of **A Philosophic Approach to Communism**, by Theodore B. Brameld. *American Economic Review* 24 (Sept. 1934): 548-49.

"A Demonstration for Relief." Letter by Hook, J. B. S. Hardman, James Burnham, Louis F. Budenz, and A. J. Muste. *New Republic* 80 (31 Oct. 1934): 340.
    Comment, ibid. 81 (14 Nov. 1934): 20.

"On Workers' Democracy." *Modern Monthly* 8 (Oct. 1934): 529-44.
    Replies by Will Herberg, "Workers' Democracy or Dictatorship? On Hook's Revival of Kautsky's Theories." *Workers Age* 3 (15 Dec. 1934): 3, 8; "Parties under Workers' Rule: An Answer to Sidney Hook's Concept of Parties in a Dictatorship." Ibid. 4 (4 May 1935): 5; "As to a Multi-Party Dictatorship: Hook Confuses Dictatorship with Bourgeois Democracy." Ibid. 4 (11 May 1935): 3.
    Response by Hook, "Manners and Morals of Apache-Radicalism." *Modern Monthly* 9 (June 1935): 215-21.
    Reply by Herberg, "Professor Hook Loses His Temper: Concluding Remarks on Hook's Misconception of Dictatorship." *Workers Age* 4 (6 July 1935): 3.

"The Importance of a Point of View, Part 1." *Social Frontier* 1 (Oct. 1934): 19-22. "Part 2." Ibid. 1 (Nov. 1934): 17-19.

"The Democratic and Dictatorial Aspects of Communism." *International Conciliation* 305 (Dec. 1934): 452-64.

"Karl Marx and Moses Hess." *New International* 1 (Dec. 1934): 140-44. [Reprinted in **From Hegel to Marx**, 1936.]

1935

"Experimental Naturalism." In **American Philosophy Today and Tomorrow**, edited by Sidney Hook and Horace M. Kallen, 205-25. New York: Lee Furman, 1935.
    [Reviewed in *Annals of the American Academy of Political and Social Science* 185 (May 1936): 251-52 (W. Rex Crawford); *Ethics* 48 (July 1938): 554-57 (Marjorie Glicksman); *Journal of Philosophy* 33 (13 Feb.

1936): 109-10 (H. A. Larrabee); *New Republic* 86 (8 Apr. 1936): 255 (Norbert Guterman); *New Scholasticism* 10 (July 1936): 292-94 (Henry A. Lucks); *Partisan Review and Anvil* 3 (Mar. 1936): 27-28 (David Ramsey); *Special Libraries* 27 (1936): 313.]

"Hegel and Marx." In **Studies in the History of Ideas**, vol. 3, 329-404. New York: Columbia University Press, 1935.
[Reprinted in **From Hegel to Marx**, 1936.]

"Marx's Criticism of 'True Socialism.'" *New International* 2 (Jan. 1935): 13-16.

"A Philosophic Pathfinder." Review of **Mind, Self and Society**, by George H. Mead. *Nation* 140 (13 Feb. 1935): 195-96.

"Interpreting Soviet Russia." Review of **Moscow Dialogues; Russian Sociology; Religion and Communism;** and **The Communist's Answer to the World's Needs**, by Julius Hecker; **The Bolshevik Revolution, 1917-1918**, by James Bunyan and H. H. Fisher; **Bolshevism, Fascism and the Liberal-Democratic State**, by Maurice Parmelee. *Saturday Review* 11 (16 Feb. 1935): 494-95.

"Plato Without the Legend." Review of **The Platonic Legend**, by Warner Fite. *New Republic* 82 (27 Feb. 1935): 81.

"A Reply to Professor Cohen." *Student Outlook* 3, no. 3 (Feb. 1935): 19-21.
Reply to Morris R. Cohen's review of **Towards the Understanding of Karl Marx**, ibid. 3, nos. 2-3 (Nov.-Dec. 1934): 31-34.
Reply by Hook, "A Reply to Professor Cohen--II." Ibid. 3, no. 5 (May 1935): 11-13.
Rejoinder by Cohen, "Cohen on Hook on Cohen on Hook." Ibid., 13-16.

"Marxism and Religion." *Modern Monthly* 9 (Mar. 1935): 29-35.

"Our Philosophers." *Current History* 41 (Mar. 1935): 698-704.

"Philosophical Burlesque: On Some Stalinist Antics in Philosophy." *Modern Monthly* 9 (May 1935): 163-72.

"What Happened in Russia." Review of **The Russian Revolution, 1917-1921**, by William Henry Chamberlin. *Saturday Review* 12 (1 June 1935): 40-41.

"Pareto's Sociological System." Review of **The Mind and Society**, by Vilfredo Pareto. *Nation* 140 (26 June 1935): 747-48.

"Middle Class Patterns of European Fascism." *Jewish Frontier* 2 (Oct. 1935): 14-18.

"Saint Stalin." Review of **Stalin**, by Henri Barbusse. *Saturday Review* 13 (16 Nov. 1935): 7.

"A Triumph of Scholarship." Review of **Encyclopaedia of the Social Sciences**. *Saturday Review* 13 (7 Dec. 1935): 38, 42.

"William James." Review of **The Thought and Character of William James**, by Ralph Barton Perry. *Nation* 141 (11 Dec. 1935): 684-87.

"Ludwig Feuerbach." Part 1. *Modern Monthly* 9 (Dec. 1935): 357-69; Part 2: "Feuerbach's Psychology of Religion." Ibid. 9 (Jan. 1936): 430-36; Part 3: "Feuerbach's Philosophy of Anthropomorphism." Ibid. 9 (Mar. 1936): 493-501.

1936

From Hegel to Marx: Studies in the Intellectual Development of Karl Marx. New York: John Day Co., 1936; New York: Reynal and Hitchcock, 1936; New York: Humanities Press, 1950.
[Reviewed in *American Sociological Review* 3 (Apr. 1938): 295-97 (Howard Becker); *Boston Evening Transcript*, 1 Aug. 1936, 4 (Sigmund Arnold Lavine); *Christian Century* 54 (3 Mar. 1937): 291; *Criterion* 16 (1937): 322-26 (A. L. Rowse); *Economist* 124 (29 Aug. 1936): 395; *Ethics* 47 (1937): 405 (Harold D. Lasswell); *International Journal of Ethics* 47 (Apr. 1937): 405-6 (Harold D. Lasswell); *Journal of Philosophy* 34 (21 Jan. 1937): 47-49 (V. J. McGill); *London Mercury* 34 (June 1936): 194; *Nation* 143 (15 Aug. 1936): 188-89 (Harold J. Laski); *New Republic* 88 (30 Sept. 1936): 232-33 (Herman Simpson); ibid. 91 (4 Aug. 1937): 366-68 (Edmund Wilson); *New Statesman and Nation*, n.s. 11 (6 June 1936): 897 (R. H. S. Crossman); *New York Herald Tribune Books*, 23 Aug. 1936, 2 (Max Lerner); *New York Times Book Review*, 6 Dec. 1936, 40 (Fabian Franklin); *Philosophical Review* 47 (Mar. 1938): 218-21 (George H. Sabine); *Saturday Review* 14 (15 Aug. 1936): 11 (Max Eastman); *Scrutiny* 5 (Dec. 1936): 306-15 (E. W. F. Tomlin); *Social Frontier* 3 (Jan. 1937): 123 (Theodore B. Brameld); *Spectator* 156 (12 June 1936): 1090 (J. P. Mayer); *Tablet* 168 (19 Dec. 1936): 878 (Christopher Dawson); *Times* (London) *Literary Supplement*, 11 July 1936, 574.]

Letter to the editor. *Fortune* 13 (Jan. 1936): 24.
    Reply to Harold G. Moulton, "Economic Progress without Economic Revolution." Ibid. 12 (Nov. 1935): 77ff.

"Revolutionary Mythology." Review of **Introduction to Dialectical Materialism**, by August Thalheimer. *Nation* 142 (4 Mar. 1936): 288-90.

"The Faith of a Scientist." Review of **Religion and Science**, by Bertrand Russell. *New Republic* 86 (1 Apr. 1936): 227.

"Marx's Life and Thought." Review of **Karl Marx: The Story of His Life**, by Franz Mehring. *Saturday Review* 13 (18 Apr. 1936): 18-19.

"Radicals and War." A debate with Ludwig Lore. *Modern Monthly* 10 (Apr. 1936): 12-17.

"Ethereal Politics." Review of **Three Gods Give an Evening to Politics**, by Richard Rothschild. *Nation* 142 (20 May 1936): 653-54.

"Social Masks and Social Facts." Review of **The Symbols of Government**, by Thurman W. Arnold. *New Republic* 87 (20 May 1936): 51-52.

"On Rereading Veblen." Review of **What Veblen Taught**, edited by Wesley Clair Mitchell. *New Republic* 87 (17 June 1936): 182.

"Man Behind Marx." Review of **Friedrich Engels**, by Gustav Mayer. *Saturday Review* 14 (27 June 1936): 10.

"The Prophetic Trotsky." Review of **The Third International After Lenin**, by Leon Trotsky. *Saturday Review* 14 (11 July 1936): 10.

"New Trend in Philosophy." Review of **Movements of Thought in the Nineteenth Century**, by George H. Mead. *Nation* 143 (22 Aug. 1936): 220-21.

"The Uses of Opposition." *Modern Monthly* 10 (Aug. 1936): 13-15.

"Understanding Karl Marx: A Debate. 2: Marxism as a Living Philosophy." *New Republic* 88 (30 Sept. 1936): 233-34.
    Reply to Herman Simpson's review of **From Hegel to Marx**, ibid., 232-33.
    Rebuttal by Simpson, ibid. 89 (18 Nov. 1936): 75-76.
    Rejoinder by Hook, ibid., 76.
    Comment by Harold J. Laski, ibid. 89 (25 Nov. 1936): 114.

"Philosophy in Russia." *Social Frontier* 3 (Oct. 1936): 24.
    Reply to Theodore B. Brameld, "Where Philosophy Counts." Ibid. 2 (June 1936): 290-91.
    Response by Brameld, ibid. 3 (Oct. 1936): 24-25.

"Philosophy in Action." Review of **The Decline and Rise of the Consumer**, by Horace M. Kallen. *Opinion* 7 (Dec. 1936): 25, 27.

1937

"The Philosophical Implications of Economic Planning." In **Planned Society: Yesterday, Today, Tomorrow,** edited by Findlay MacKenzie, 663-77. New York: Prentice-Hall, 1937.

Introduction to **What is Folksocialism? A Critical Analysis,** by Paul Sering, 7-11. New York: League for Industrial Democracy, 1937.

"Marxism and Values." *Marxist Quarterly* 1 (Jan.-Mar. 1937): 238-45. [Reprinted in **Reason, Social Myths, and Democracy,** 1940.]

Review of **Wandlungen der Weltanshauung,** by Karl Joël. *Journal of Philosophy* 34 (4 Mar. 1937): 131-33.

"Dialectic and Nature." *Marxist Quarterly* 1 (Apr.-June 1937): 253-84.

"A Philosopher on Movie Censorship." Review of **Art and Prudence: A Study in Practical Philosophy**, by Mortimer J. Adler. *Saturday Review* 16 (15 May 1937): 17.

"Both Their Houses." *New Republic* 91 (2 June 1937): 104.
Reply to Malcolm Cowley's review of **The Case of the Anti-Soviet Trotskyite Center.** Ibid. 90 (7 Apr. 1937): 267-70.

"History in Swing Rhythm." Review of **Social and Cultural Dynamics,** by Pitirim A. Sorokin. *Nation* 145 (10 July 1937): 48-49.

"Socialism for a Democracy." Review of **American Socialism,** by Harry W. Laidler. *Saturday Review* 16 (28 Aug. 1937): 20.

"Fantasia on the Left." Review of **The Conquest of Power: Liberalism, Anarchism, Syndicalism, Socialism, Fascism, and Communism,** by Albert Weisbord. *Nation* 145 (11 Sept. 1937): 270-71.

"Discussion: Totalitarianism in Education." *Social Research* 4 (Sept. 1937): 401-4.

"Seeking Truth about Trotsky." Review of **The Case of Leon Trotsky: Report of Hearings on the Charges Made Against Him in the Moscow Trials,** by John Dewey et al. *New York Herald Tribune Books*, 10 Oct.

1937, 8.

"Worlds of Chance." Review of **A World of Chance**, by Edward Gleason
Spaulding. *Nation* 145 (23 Oct. 1937): 451-53.

"Promise without Dogma: A Social Philosophy for Jews." *Menorah Journal*
25 (Oct.-Dec. 1937): 273-88.
  Reply by Alvin Johnson, "A Social Philosophy for Jews." Ibid. 26
   (Jan.-Mar. 1938): 1-6.
  Response by Hook, "A Note on Alvin Johnson's Article." Ibid.,
   103-4.

"The Sociology of Knowledge." Review of **Ideology and Utopia**, by Karl
Mannheim. *Marxist Quarterly* 1 (Oct.-Dec. 1937): 450-54.
[Reprinted in **Reason, Social Myths, and Democracy**, 1940.]

"The Technique of Mystification." Review of **Attitudes toward History**, by
Kenneth Burke. *Partisan Review* 4 (Dec. 1937): 57-62.
  Reply by Burke, "Is Mr. Hook a Socialist?" Ibid. 4 (Jan. 1938): 40-44.
  Response by Hook, "Is Mr. Burke Serious?" Ibid., 44-47.

"Ends and Means." Review of **Ends and Means**, by Aldous Huxley. *Nation*
145 (11 Dec. 1937): 656, 658.

"Liberalism and the Case of Leon Trotsky." *Southern Review* 3 (1937-38):
267-82.
  Reply to Frederick L. Schuman, "Leon Trotsky: Martyr or
   Renegade?" Ibid., 51-74.
  Comments on Schuman by Malcolm Cowley, Max Eastman,
   John Dewey, Carleton Beals, and James T. Farrell, ibid., 199-
   208.
  Reply to Beals, ibid., 406-10.
  Response by Beals, ibid., 410-11.
  Reply by Schuman, ibid., 411-15.
  Response by Hook, ibid., 415.
  Response by Farrell, ibid., 415-16.

1938

"Violence: As a (Marxist) Professor Sees It." *Common Sense* 7 (Jan. 1938):
22-23.

"The Ways of Philosophy." Review of **Four Ways of Philosophy**, by Irwin
Edman. *Nation* 146 (8 Jan. 1938): 48-49.

"Storm Signals in American Philosophy." *Virginia Quarterly Review* 14 (Winter 1938): 29-43.

"Zweiter Entfer oyf der Frage: Zie Leybt in sich Izt die Sowietische Arbeiter Besser, wie die Arbeiter in andere Lender?" *Der Tog*, 7 Feb. 1938, 5.

"Broun v. Dewey." *New Republic* 94 (16 Feb. 1938): 48.
    Partial letter in reply to Heywood Broun, "Dr. Dewey Finds Communists in the CIO." Ibid. 93 (12 Jan. 1938): 280-81.
    Editorial comment, ibid. 94 (2 Mar. 1938): 105.
    Complete letter, "How New Republic Lives Up to Its Liberal Creed." *Workers Age* 7 (26 Feb. 1938): 6.

"Metaphysics and Social Attitudes: A Reply." *Social Frontier* 4 (Feb. 1938): 153-58.
    Reply to Brand Blanshard, "Metaphysics and Social Attitudes." Ibid. 4 (Dec. 1937): 79-81.
    Response by Pitirim A. Sorokin, "Metaphysics and Social Attitudes: Some Forgotten Facts." Ibid. 4 (Mar. 1938): 179-80.
    Rejoinder by Blanshard, "Metaphysics and Social Attitudes: A Rejoinder." Ibid. 4 (Apr. 1938): 219-21.
    Response by Hook, "Relevant Issues Restated." Ibid., 221-23.

"Logic, Politics, and Plain Decency." *Social Frontier* 4 (Mar. 1938): 190-92.
    Response to Earl Browder, "Toward the American Commonwealth: II. The Present Communist Position." Ibid. 4 (Feb. 1938): 161-64.

"Corliss Lamont: 'Friend of the G.P.U.'" *Modern Monthly* 10 (Mar. 1938): 5-8.

"The Baptism of Aristotle and Marx." Review of **What Man Has Made of Man**, by Mortimer J. Adler. *Nation* 146 (9 Apr. 1938): 415-17.

"Some Social Uses and Abuses of Semantics." *Partisan Review* 4 (Apr. 1938): 14-25.

"The Politician's Handbook." Review of **The Folklore of Capitalism**, by Thurman W. Arnold. *University of Chicago Law Review* 5 (Apr. 1938): 341-49.
    Reply by Arnold, "The Folklore of Mr. Hook--A Reply." Ibid., 349-53.
    Rejoinder by Hook, "Neither Myth nor Power--A Rejoinder." Ibid., 354-57.
  [Reprinted in **Reason, Social Myths, and Democracy**, 1940.]

"Thoughts in Season." *Socialist Review* 6 (May-June 1938): 6-7, 16.

"Charges Against Trotsky." Review of **Not Guilty: Report of the Commission of Inquiry into the Charges Made against Leon Trotsky in the Moscow Trials,** by John Dewey et al. *New York Herald Tribune Books,* 24 July 1938, 6.

"Democracy as a Way of Life." *Southern Review* 4 (Summer 1938): 45-57. Revised as "The Democratic Way of Life." *Menorah Journal* 26 (Oct.-Dec. 1938): 261-75.

"Science and the New Obscurantism." *Modern Quarterly* 11 (Fall 1938): 66-85.

"Eduard Heimann on the 'Revolutionary Situation.'" *Social Research* 5 (Nov. 1938): 464-71.
    Response to Heimann, "The 'Revolutionary Situation' and the Middle Classes." Ibid. 5 (May 1938): 227-36.
    Reply by Heimann, ibid. 5 (Nov. 1938): 471-73.

"The Tragedy of German Jewry." *New Leader* 21 (26 Nov. 1938): 8.

"Dialectic in Social and Historical Inquiry." *Journal of Philosophy* 35 (8 Dec. 1938): 683-84.

"Whitehead's Latest Phase." Review of **Modes of Thought,** by Alfred North Whitehead. *Nation* 147 (10 Dec. 1938): 632-33.

"Critical Analysis as a Method of Radio Education." *School and Society* 48 (31 Dec. 1938): 858-59.

1939

John Dewey: An Intellectual Portrait. New York: John Day Co., 1939.
[Reviewed in *Booklist* 36 (1 Dec. 1939): 125; *Journal of Higher Education* 11 (Apr. 1940): 226-29 (Boyd H. Bode); *Journal of Philosophy* 36 (7 Dec. 1939): 695 (Herbert Schneider); *Kenyon Review* 2 (Winter 1940): 121-22 (Philip Blair Rice); *Nation* 150 (6 Jan. 1940): 22-23 (Eliseo Vivas); *New Leader* 22 (16 Dec. 1939): 2 (John L. Childs); *New Republic* 101 (6 Dec. 1939): 206-7 (Paul Weiss); *New York Herald Tribune Books,* 5 Nov. 1939, 2 (Ernest Sutherland Bates); *Partisan Review* 7 (1940): 62-67 (Morton G. White); *Philosophical Review* 50 (Jan. 1941): 86-87 (Everett Wesley Hall); *Saturday Review* 21 (11 Nov. 1939): 12-13 (Robert Bierstedt); *Southern Review* 5 (1939): 700-710 (William Barrett); *Thought* 15 (June 1940): 365-67 (Ruth Byrns).]

"A Challenge to the Liberal-Arts College." *Journal of Higher Education* 10 (Jan. 1939): 14-23, 58.
[Reprinted in **Education and the Taming of Power**, 1973.]

"The Fetishism of Power." Review of **The Ruling Classes**, by Gaetano Mosca. *Nation* 148 (13 May 1939): 562-63.

All Totalitarianism Opposed." *New York Times*, 17 May 1939, 22.

Letter by Hook introducing the Manifesto of the Committee for Cultural Freedom. Manifesto signed by Hook et al. *Nation* 148 (27 May 1939): 626.
Reply by Freda Kirchwey, "Red Totalitarianism." Ibid., 605-6.
Response by Hook, ibid. 148 (17 June 1939): 710.
Rebuttal by Kirchwey, ibid., 711.

"The Anatomy of the Popular Front." Review of **It Is Later Than You Think,** by Max Lerner. *Partisan Review* 6 (Spring 1939): 29-45.

"Soviet Union a Totalitarian Dictatorship Just as Is Germany." Letter to the editor. *New York Post*, 7 June 1939, 12.

"Hook Warns Against Forgery Tactics of Totalitarian Agents." Letter to the editor. *New Leader* 22 (24 June 1939): 8.

"Dialectic in Social and Historical Inquiry." *Journal of Philosophy* 36 (6 July 1939): 365-78.

"'The Totalitarian Mind'--and Those Who Hew to the 'Line.'" *New York Post*, 2 Sept. 1939, 12.

"Fight for Civil Liberties Can Balk 'Totalitarianites.'" Debate with Max Nomad entitled "Which Way the Fight on Fascism?" *New Leader* 22 (7 Oct. 1939): 5.
Response to Nomad, "Fight on Status Quo Best Weapon Against Fascism." Ibid. 22 (2 Sept. 1939): 7, 10.
Rebuttal by Nomad, "Only 'Bread and Butter' Campaign Will Swing Masses Against Fascists." Ibid., 5, 7.

"John Dewey at Eighty." *New Leader* 22 (28 Oct. 1939): 5.

"The Importance of John Dewey in Modern Thought." *Modern Quarterly* 11 (Fall 1939): 30-35.

"Salute to John Dewey!" *Call* 5 (4 Nov. 1939): 4.
Response by Upton Sinclair, ibid. 5 (11 Nov. 1939): 4.

Reply by Hook, ibid.

"Hook Urges Inclusion of Ludlow Clause in Neutrality Act." *New Leader* 22 (4 Nov. 1939): 8.

"Upton Sinclair vs. Sidney Hook: The Debate on Russia Grows Warmer." *Call* 5 (18 Nov. 1939): 4.
> Exchange between Hook and Sinclair, "Hook Can't Rule Me Out!" Ibid.

"The Art of Crypto-Stalinism: Its Theory and Practice." *New Leader* 22 (18 Nov. 1939): 5, 8.
> Exchange between Hook and George Soule, "USSR and The New Republic." Ibid. 22 (16 Dec. 1939): 5.
> Comments by Leon Dennen, "Notes on Crypto-Stalinism." Ibid. 22 (23 Dec. 1939): 8, 7.

"CCF Protests Jailing of French Pacifists." *New Leader* 22 (23 Dec. 1939): 7.

"Academic Freedom and 'The Trojan Horse' in American Education." *American Association of University Professors Bulletin* 25 (Dec. 1939): 550-55.

"Reflections on the Russian Revolution." Review of **The Revolution Betrayed**, by Leon Trotsky. *Southern Review* 4 (Winter 1939): 429-62.

Review of **Principles of the Theory of Probability**, by Ernest Nagel. *Philosophic Abstracts* 1 (1939-40): 3.

Review of **The Philosophy of John Dewey, A Critical Study**, by Folke Leander. *Philosophic Abstracts* 1 (1939-40): 21-22.

"Abstractions in Social Inquiry." *Illinois Law Review* 34 (1939-40): 15-29. [Reprinted in **Reason, Social Myths, and Democracy**, 1940.]

1940

Reason, Social Myths, and Democracy. New York: John Day Co., 1940. [Reviewed in *Annals of the American Academy of Political and Social Science* 213 (Jan. 1941): 199-200 (Hans Kohn); *Ethics* 52 (Apr. 1942): 386-87 (Glenn Negley); *Frontiers of Democracy* 7 (15 Jan. 1941): 123-25 (John L. Childs); *Journal of Philosophy* 38 (24 Apr. 1941): 243-49 (V. J. McGill); *Library Journal* 65 (15 Oct. 1940): 873 (Felix E. Hirsch); *Living Age* 359 (Feb. 1941): 593-95 (Albert Lippman); *Nation* 151 (19 Oct.

1940): 370-71 (Reinhold Niebuhr); *New Leader* 24 (11 Jan. 1941): 5, 7 (John L. Childs); *New Republic* 103 (2 Dec. 1940): 762-64 (Irwin Edman); *New Yorker* 16 (7 Dec. 1940): 105; *New York Herald Tribune Books*, 22 Dec. 1940, 6 (A. N. Holcombe); *Partisan Review* 8 (Jan.-Feb. 1941): 69-72 (Bertram D. Wolfe); *Personalist* 23 (July 1942): 305-6 (Ralph Tyler Flewelling); *Philosophical Review* 51 (July 1942): 427-32 (Albert R. Chandler); *Saturday Review* 23 (11 Jan. 1941): 15 (Jacques Barzun).]

"Unreconstructed Fellow-Travelers." *Call*, 13 Jan. 1940, 2.

Review of **Hegel: Sein Wollen und Sein Werk**, vol. 2, by Theodor L. Haering. *Philosophical Review* 49 (Jan. 1940): 87-88.

"An Attack on Freedom." *New York Herald Tribune*, 9 Mar. 1940, 14.

"Socialists Face Need of Unified Action." *New Leader* 23 (9 Mar. 1940): 7.

"Conceptions of Human Motivation: Socialism and the Motives of Men." *Frontiers of Democracy* 6 (15 Mar. 1940): 167.

"On Ideas." Review of **Ideas Are Weapons**, by Max Lerner. *Partisan Review* 7 (Mar.-Apr. 1940): 152-60.
[Reprinted in **Reason, Social Myths, and Democracy**, 1940.]

"What Stalin Wrote." Review of **Stalin's Kampf: Joseph Stalin's Credo**, edited by M. R. Werner. *New York Herald Tribune Books*, 7 Apr. 1940, 6.

"Prof. Hook to Prof. Schuman." *Saturday Review* 22 (20 Apr. 1940): 9.
Reply to Frederick L. Schuman's review of **Stalin's Kampf: Joseph Stalin's Credo**, edited by M. R. Werner, ibid. 22 (6 Apr. 1940): 10, 29.

"What Is Living and What Is Dead in Marxism?" *Frontiers of Democracy* 6 (15 Apr. 1940): 218-20.

"The Integral Humanism of Jacques Maritain." Review of **True Humanism**, by Jacques Maritain. *Partisan Review* 7 (May-June 1940): 204-29.
[Reprinted in **Reason, Social Myths, and Democracy**, 1940.]

"Is Nazism a Social Revolution?" *New Leader* 23 (20 July 1940): 4, 6.

"How Has John Strachey Changed His Mind?" Review of **A Programme for Progress**, by John Strachey. *New York Herald Tribune Books*, 21 July 1940, 5.

"Socialism, Common Sense and the War." *New Leader* 23 (31 Aug. 1940): 7.
    Reply by Henry Pinski, "Hook's Analysis Brings FDR Vote." Ibid.
    23 (14 Sept. 1940): 8.

"Alexander Goldenweiser: Three Tributes." With Ruth Benedict and
    Margaret Mead. *Modern Quarterly* 11 (Summer 1940): 31-32.

Review of **Positive Democracy**, by James Feibleman. *Journal of Philosophy*
    37 (26 Sept. 1940): 557-59.

"Thinkers Who Prepared for Revolution." Review of **To the Finland Sta-
    tion: A Study in the Writing and Acting of History**, by Edmund Wilson.
    New York Herald Tribune Books, 29 Sept. 1940, 5.

"Engels as Scientist." Review of **Dialectics of Nature**, by Friedrich Engels.
    Nation 151 (5 Oct. 1940): 308.

"Planning--and Freedom." Review of **Man and Society in an Age of
    Reconstruction**, by Karl Mannheim. *Nation* 151 (26 Oct. 1940): 398-99.

"The New Medievalism." *New Republic* 103 (28 Oct. 1940): 602-6.
    Hook's comments on Mortimer J. Adler's "God and the Professors." A
    paper delivered at the national Conference on Science, Philosophy, and
    Religion in their relation to the Democratic Way of Life. Jewish
    Theological Seminary, New York City, 10-11 Sept. 1940. Adler's and
    Hook's papers reprinted in a special issue of the *Daily Maroon* (Univ-
    ersity of Chicago), 14 Nov. 1940, 1-4.

"Metaphysics, War, and the Intellectuals." Review of **Chart for Rough
    Water**, by Waldo Frank; **The Irresponsibles**, by Archibald MacLeish;
    and **Faith for Living**, by Lewis Mumford. *Menorah Journal* 28 (Oct.
    1940): 326-37.

"Despair on Mt. Olympus." Review of **The Realm of Spirit**, by George
    Santayana. *Nation* 151 (2 Nov. 1940): 423-24.

"A Democratic Survival." Review of **State of the Masses**, by Emil Lederer.
    New York Herald Tribune Books, 1 Dec. 1940, 38.

1941

"'Out of the Night' Uncovers Underworld of a Rotted Religion." Review of
    Out of the Night, by Jan Valtin. *New Leader* 24 (15 Feb. 1941): 5.

"The Counter-Reformation in American Education." *Antioch Review* 1

(Mar. 1941): 109-16.

"The Basic Values and Loyalties of Communism." *American Teacher* 25 (May 1941): 4-6.

"Reason and Revolution." Review of **Reason and Revolution: Hegel and the Rise of Social Theory**, by Herbert Marcuse. *New Republic* 105 (21 July 1941): 90-91.

"Moscow Order Dissolving Communist Party in U.S. Would Swing Wide Public Support to Aid for U.S.S.R." *New Leader* 24 (11 Oct. 1941): 4.

"Russia's Democracy Denied." *New York Times*, 29 Oct. 1941, 22.
Reply to Albert A. Volk, "Democracy Is Discussed." Ibid., 22 Oct. 1941, 22.

"Social Change and Original Sin: Answer to Niebuhr." Review of **The Nature and Destiny of Man**, by Reinhold Niebuhr and **Man on His Nature**, by Charles Sherrington. *New Leader* 24 (8 Nov. 1941): 5, 7.

"The Late Mr. Tate." *Southern Review* 6 (1941): 840-43.

1942

"Salvation by Semantics." Review of **Language in Action: A Guide to Accurate Thinking**, by S. I. Hayakawa. *Nation* 154 (3 Jan. 1942): 16.

"Crisis of Our Culture." Review of **The Crisis of Our Age: The Social and Cultural Outlook**, by Pitirim A. Sorokin. *New York Herald Tribune Books*, 11 Jan. 1942, 10.

"Russia's Military Successes Do Not Whitewash Crimes at Home." *New Leader* 25 (31 Jan. 1942): 5.

"National Unity and 'Corporate Thinking.'" *Menorah Journal* 30 (Jan. 1942): 61-68. Comments on **Science, Philosophy and Religion: Second Symposium** (New York, 1942).

Review of **Design for Power**, by Frederick L. Schuman. *Partisan Review* 9 (Mar.-Apr. 1942): 169.

"Milton Mayer: Fake Jeremiah." *New Leader* 25 (4 Apr. 1942): 5.

"Whitehead's Final Views." Review of **The Philosophy of Alfred North Whitehead**, edited by Paul A. Schilpp. *Nation* 154 (4 Apr. 1942): 401-3.

"The Philosophical Presuppositions of Democracy." *Ethics* 52 (Apr. 1942): 275-96.

"Two Views on Mortimer Adler and Milton Mayer." With Francis McMahon. *New Leader* 25 (16 May 1942): 5, 7.

"Sidney Hook Analyzes a New 'Faith' for the Businessman: A Review of Hocking's New 'Philosophical Healing.'" Review of **What Man Can Make of Man**, by William Ernest Hocking. *New Leader* 25 (5 Sept. 1942): 2, 7.

"The Function of Higher Education in Postwar Reconstruction." *Journal of Educational Sociology* 16 (Sept. 1942): 43-51.

"Legitimacy and Revolution." Review of **The Principles of Power: The Great Political Crises of History**, by Guglielmo Ferrero. *New Republic* 107 (19 Oct. 1942): 508, 510, 512.

"Theological Tom-Tom and Metaphysical Bagpipe." *Humanist* 2 (Autumn 1942): 96-102.
> Replies by Edwin E. Aubrey, W. F. Albright, R. L. Calhoun, H. A. Overstreet, George Boas, Max C. Otto, and Horace M. Kallen, ibid. 3 (Spring 1943): 24-32.
> Response by Hook, ibid., 32-38.

1943

The Hero in History: A Study in Limitation and Possibility. New York: John Day Co., 1943; Boston: Beacon Press, 1955.
[Reviewed in *Annals of the American Academy of Political and Social Science* 229 (Sept. 1943): 197-98 (Glenn R. Morrow); *Atlantic Monthly* 172 (July 1943): 129; *Booklist* 39 (1 June 1943): 385; *Catholic Historical Review* 30 (Apr. 1944): 59 (Geoffrey Bruun); *Ethics* 54 (Jan. 1944): 152-53 (Albert William Levi); *Foreign Affairs* 22 (Oct. 1943): 155 (Robert Gale Woolbert); *Frontiers of Democracy* 10 (15 Dec. 1943): 98-99 (George Freimarck); *Historical Bulletin* 34 (May 1956): 246 (Crane Brinton); *Journal of Philosophy* 40 (14 Oct. 1943): 575-80 (John Herman Randall, Jr.); *Kenyon Review* 6 (Winter 1944): 126-29 (Delmore Schwartz); *Nation* 157 (18 Sept. 1943): 326-28 (Jacques Barzun); *New Republic* 108 (21 June 1943): 834-35 (C. Wright Mills); *New Yorker* 19 (1 May 1943): 67; *New York Herald Tribune Weekly Book Review*, 6 June 1943, 16 (Adrienne Koch); *New York Times*, 22 Apr. 1943, 27 (John Chamberlain); *New York Times Book Review*, 27 June 1943, 23 (Joseph Freeman); ibid., 16 Oct. 1955, 36 (Harvey Breit); *Philosophical Review* 53 (Jan. 1944): 76-77 (Carl Becker); *Saturday Review* 26 (1 May 1943): 6

(Robert Pick); *School and Society* 57 (24 Apr. 1943): 484; *Sewanee Review* 51 (1943): 606-10 (Monroe C. Beardsley); *Social Studies* 34 (Dec. 1943): 376 (Walter H. Mohr); *Spectator* (London) 174 (1945): 316 (Richard Rumbold); *Tablet* 185 (26 May 1945): 250; *Time* 41 (17 May 1943): 90, 92.]

"The New Failure of Nerve, Part 1." *Partisan Review* 10 (Jan.-Feb. 1943): 2-23; "Part 2: The Failure of the Left." Ibid. 10 (Mar.-Apr. 1943): 165-77.
> Responses by Erasmus Minor, Robert Fitzgerald, E. S. Spachman, and Robert W. Flint, ibid., 204-6.
> Reply by Hook, ibid., 206-8.
> Response by Newton Arvin, ibid., 208.
> Response by William Ferry, "Other People's Nerve." *Enquiry* 1 (May 1943): 3-6.
> Response by David Merian, "The Nerve of Sidney Hook." *Partisan Review* 10 (May-June 1943): 248-57.
> Reply by Hook, "The Politics of Wonderland." Ibid., 258-62.
> Reply by Merian, "Socialism and the Failure of Nerve--The Controversy Continued." Ibid. 10 (Sept.-Oct. 1943): 473-76.
> Reply by Hook, "Faith, Hope, and Dialectic: Merian in Wonderland." Ibid., 476-81.
> Response by M. Morrison, "Sidney Hook's Attack on Trotskyism." *Fourth International* 4 (July 1943): 212-15.
> Response by Malcolm Cowley, "Marginalia." *New Republic* 109 (12 July 1943): 50.
> Response by Isaac Rosenfeld, "The Failure of Verve." Ibid. 109 (19 July 1943): 80-81.
> Reply by Hook, "Experience and Intelligence." Ibid. 109 (6 Sept. 1943): 336-37.
> Responses by Cowley and Rosenfeld, ibid., 337-38.
> [Reprinted in **The Quest for Being**, 1961.]

"Education for the New Order." Review of **Education Between Two Worlds**, by Alexander Meiklejohn. *Nation* 156 (27 Feb. 1943): 308, 310, 312.
> Response by Mark Van Doren, ibid. 156 (20 Mar. 1943): 430.
> Rebuttal by Hook, ibid., 430-31.

"A Critique: The Elite and the Masses." *New Leader* 26 (20 Mar. 1943): 5.

"Tribute to Carlo Tresca." *Il Martello* 28 (28 Mar. 1943): 44.

"Law, Freedom, and Human Action." *New Leader* 26 (3 Apr. 1943): 4, 6.

"Old and New Roads to Freedom." *New Leader* 26 (10 Apr. 1943): 4-6;

ibid. (17 Apr. 1943): 4.

"Philosophy of Art and Culture." Review of **Art and Freedom**, by Horace
M. Kallen. *New York Herald Tribune Weekly Book Review*, 11 Apr. 1943,
20.

"A National Scandal--Critics Hit 'Submission to Moscow.'" Prepared statement on the movie *Mission to Moscow*. *New Leader* 26 (8 May 1943): 2.

"Stalin Liquidates the Communist International." *New Leader* 26 (29 May
1943): 5, 7.

"Can We Take Freedom to the Rest of the World?" *Town Meeting* 9 (23
Sept. 1943): 3-14; "Questions, Please!" Ibid., 14-21.
[Hook and Dixon Ryan Fox, Interrogators; Reinhold Niebuhr and
Robert A. Taft, Speakers.]

"Illusions of Our Time." Review of **Reflections on the Revolution of Our
Time**, by Harold J. Laski. *Partisan Review* 10 (Sept.-Oct. 1943): 442-
47.

"Socialism and Sewage System." Review of **Development of Collective
Enterprise**, by Seba Eldridge et al. *New Leader* 26 (9 Oct. 1943): 3.

"Charles Beard's Political Testament." Review of **The Republic: Conversation on Fundamentals**, by Charles A. Beard. *Nation* 157 (23 Oct. 1943):
474-76.

"The Perpetual Debate." Review of **Majority Rule and Minority Rights**, by
Henry Steele Commager. *Nation* 157 (11 Dec. 1943): 709-10.

1944

"Naturalism and Democracy." In **Naturalism and the Human Spirit**, edited
by Yervant H. Krikorian, 40-64. New York: Columbia University Press,
1944.

"The Rebirth of Political Credulity." *New Leader* 27 (1 Jan. 1944): 4-5.
Comment by William E. Bohn, "The Home Front." Ibid. 28 (6 Jan.
1945): 9.

"Humanism and the Labor Movement." *New Europe* 4 (Feb. 1944): 4-5.

"Progressive Liberal Education." Review of **Vitalizing Liberal Education**,
by Algo D. Henderson. *Nation* 158 (11 Mar. 1944): 312-14.

"Hitlerism: A Non-Metaphysical View." Review of **Der Fuehrer,** by Konrad Heiden. *Contemporary Jewish Record* 7 (Apr. 1944): 146-55.

"Ballyhoo at St. Johns College--Education in Retreat." Part 1. *New Leader* 27 (27 May 1944): 8-9.
    Reply by Edith Gordon, "Seminar at St. Johns--A Report on Adult Education in 'Practice.'" Ibid. 27 (10 June 1944): 14.

"Ballyhoo at St. Johns--II. The 'Great Books' and Progressive Teaching." Part 2. *New Leader* 27 (3 June 1944): 8-10.

"God, Geometry and the Good Society." Review of **Liberal Education**, by Mark Van Doren. *Partisan Review* 11 (Spring 1944): 161-67.

"Thirteen Arrows against Progressive Liberal Education." *Humanist* 4 (Spring 1944): 1-10.

"Heroic Vitalism." Review of **A Century of Hero-Worship**, by Eric Russell Bentley. *Nation* 159 (7 Oct. 1944): 412-14.

"What Is the Future of Democratic Socialism?" *New Leader* 27 (14 Oct. 1944): 8-9.
    Reply by Max Eastman, "1. The Notion of Democratic Socialism: Is Free Enterprise the Only Firm Guarantee of Political Freedom?" Ibid. 28 (27 Jan. 1945): 5-6; "2. The Notion of Democratic Socialism: Forward from Marxism, Not Backward to Utopianism." Ibid. 28 (3 Feb. 1945): 8; "3. The Notion of Democratic Socialism: Can Planned Economy and Private Enterprise Co-Exist?" Ibid. 28 (10 Feb. 1945): 5.
    Response by Hook, "Freedom and Socialism: Democracy and Planning Can Coexist--A Reply to Max Eastman." Ibid. 28 (3 Mar. 1945): 4-6.
[Reprinted in **Political Power and Personal Freedom**, 1959.]

"If Only . . ." Review of **Omnipotent Government**, by Ludwig von Mises. *Nation* 159 (28 Oct. 1944): 530.

"Planned Diversity." Review of **Diagnosis of Our Time**, by Karl Mannheim. *Nation* 159 (11 Nov. 1944): 596.

"An Apologist for St. John's College." *New Leader* 27 (25 Nov. 1944): 3.

"Schooling for Democrats." Review of **Your School, Your Children**, by Marie Syrkin. *Nation* 159 (18 Nov. 1944): 621-22.

"The Ends of Education." *Journal of Educational Sociology* 18 (Nov. 1944):

173-84.

"Road to Freedom." Review of **Freedom and Civilization,** by Bronislaw
Malinowski. *New Europe* 4 (Dec. 1944): 32-33.

1945

"Democracy and Education. I: Introduction." In **The Authoritarian
Attempt to Capture Education,** 10-12. Papers from the 2d Conference
on the Scientific Spirit and Democratic Faith. New York: King's Crown
Press, 1945.
[Reviewed in *America* 73 (28 July 1945): 340-41 (Allan P. Farrell);
Christian Century 62 (1 Aug. 1945): 884-85 (Edward Scribner Ames);
Commonweal 42 (29 June 1945): 268 (Leo Camp); *Journal of Philosophy*
42 (27 Sept. 1945): 548-50 (Harold Atkins Larrabee); *Nation* 161 (6 Oct.
1945): 341 (Gail Kennedy); *New York Times Book Review*, 12 Aug. 1945,
16, 18 (Benjamin Fine); *Saturday Review* 28 (23 June 1945): xxv, 37
(Ordway Tead); *Survey Graphic* 34 (Nov. 1945): 451-52 (W. Carson
Ryan).]

"The Dilemma of T. S. Eliot." *Nation* 160 (20 Jan. 1945): 69-71.
    Reply by Jacques Maritain, ibid. 160 (21 Apr. 1945): 440-42.
[Reprinted in **Philosophy and Public Policy,** 1980.]

"The Degradation of the Word." *New Leader* 28 (27 Jan. 1945): 7.
[Reprinted in **Political Power and Personal Freedom,** 1959.]

"Democratic Faith and Puritan Piety." Review of **Puritanism and Democracy,** by Ralph Barton Perry. *Nation* 160 (26 May 1945): 603-5.

"Total Condemnation: Denunciation of All Germans Held Unfair to Anti-
Nazis." Letter by Hook et al. *New York Times,* 10 June 1945, 8.
    Reply by Eleanor J. Pfund, "Disagrees on German People." Ibid., 14
    June 1945, 18.
    Reply by Arthur A. Siegbert, "Nazi Election Held Legal." Ibid., 15
    June 1945, 18.

"Man and the Universe of Symbols." Review of **An Essay on Man,** by Ernst
Cassirer. *Kenyon Review* 7 (Spring 1945): 335-38.

"The Case for Progressive Education." *Saturday Evening Post* 217 (30 June
1945): 28-29, 39, 41.

"A Discussion of the Theory of International Relations." *Journal of
Philosophy* 42 (30 Aug. 1945): 493-95.

"Are Naturalists Materialists?" With Ernest Nagel and John Dewey. *Journal of Philosophy* 42 (13 Sept. 1945): 515-30.
>Reply to Wilmon Henry Sheldon, "A Critique of Naturalism." Ibid. 42 (10 May 1945): 253-70.
>For a continuation of the discussion, see Rudolf Allers, "Does Human Nature Change?" *Catholic University Bulletin* 14, no. 2 (1946): 6-9.

"Hitler's Spirit Still Lives: Czechoslovaks Perpetrate Atrocities Against Sudeten Germans." *New Leader* 28 (6 Oct. 1945): 8.
>Reply by Alexander Boker, ibid. 28 (15 Dec. 1945): 11.

"Education for Vocation." *Antioch Review* 5 (Fall 1945): 415-28.

"The Signs of Aldous Huxley." Review of **The Perennial Philosophy**, by Aldous Huxley. *Saturday Review* 28 (3 Nov. 1945): 12-13.

"Reflections on the Nuremberg Trial." *New Leader* 28 (17 Nov. 1945): 8, 14.
>Reply by Joseph Steiner, "The Purpose of the Nuremberg Trial." Ibid. 28 (15 Dec. 1945): 11.
>Response by Hook, ibid.

"Bertrand Russell among the Sages." Review of **A History of Western Philosophy**, by Bertrand Russell. *Nation* 161 (1 Dec. 1945): 586, 588, 590.

"The Autonomy of Democratic Faith." *American Scholar* 15 (Winter 1945-46): 105-9. Part 3 of a forum on "The Future of Religion." For parts 1 and 2, see Raphael Demos, "The Need for Religion and Its Truth," 97-102, and Paul Tillich, "Vertical and Horizontal Thinking," 102-5.
>Reply by Demos, ibid., 109-10.
>Reply by Tillich, ibid., 110-12.
>Reply by Hook, ibid., 112-13.
[Reprinted in **Philosophy and Public Policy**, 1980.]

1946

Education for Modern Man. New York: Dial Press, 1946.
>[Reviewed in *Best Sellers* 6 (15 May 1946): 27-28 (Edward V. Stanford); *Booklist* 42 (15 May 1946): 293; *Catholic Educational Review* 44 (Sept. 1946): 442-45 (George F. Burnell); *Chicago Sun Book Week*, 21 Apr. 1946, 5 (Wendell Johnson); *College and University* 23 (Jan. 1948): 302-5 (T. R. McConnell); *Commentary* 2 (Oct. 1946): 397-98 (Sidney Morgenbesser); *Current History* n.s. 11 (July 1946): 49 (Roy Hillbrook); *Ethics* 58

(Jan. 1948): 133-37 (Donald Meiklejohn); *High Points* 29 (Mar. 1947): 69-73 (Ben Houseman); *Journal of Educational Psychology* 37 (Oct. 1946): 442-45 (Melvin G. Rigg); *Journal of Higher Education* 17 (June 1946): 332-33 (Stringfellow Barr); ibid., 332-34 (C. H. Gray); *Journal of Philosophy* 43 (7 Nov. 1946): 629-36 (Mason W. Gross); *Kirkus* 14 (1 Apr. 1946): 171; *Library Journal* 71 (15 Apr. 1946): 584 (Thelma Brackett); *Madison Quarterly* 7 (Mar. 1947): 84 (Ethel Garber); *Mental Hygiene* 31 (Apr. 1947): 309-12 (Henry Neumann); *Nation* 162 (20 Apr. 1946): 476, 478 (Irwin Edman); *New Leader* 29 (25 May 1946): 11 (Eduard C. Lindeman); *New Republic* 114 (10 June 1946): 840-41 (Jerome Nathanson); *New Yorker* 22 (18 May 1946): 110; *New York Herald Tribune Weekly Book Review*, 11 Aug. 1946, 10 (Albert Guerard); *New York Times*, 26 May 1946, 6 (Howard Mumford Jones); *Partisan Review* 13 (Nov.-Dec. 1946): 595-96 (Delmore Schwartz); *Philosophical Review* 56 (1947): 88-90 (Henry M. Wriston); *Progressive Education* 24 (Jan. 1946): 95, 107-8 (Ursula Reinhardt); *Review of Politics* 9 (Oct. 1947): 502-4 (Leo R. Ward); *Saturday Review* 29 (20 Apr. 1946): 22 (Eric Russell Bentley); *School and Society* 65 (22 Mar. 1947): 209-10 (William Sener Rusk); *Sewanee Review* 55 (1947): 170-72 (Herbert Marshall McLuhan); *Time* 47 (6 May 1946): 88; *U.S. Quarterly Book List* 2 (Sept. 1946): 210; *Western Review* 11 (Winter 1947): 59-71 (Eliseo Vivas).]

"Illustrations." In **Theory and Practice in Historical Study: A Report of the Committee on Historiography**, 108-30. New York: Social Science Research Council (Bulletin 54), 1946.
[With "The Need for Greater Precision in the Use of Historical Terms," by Charles A. Beard. Ibid., 105-8.]

"Introduction." In **Social Democracy Versus Communism**, by Karl Kautsky, edited and translated by David Shub and Joseph Shaplen, 7-20. New York: Rand School Press, 1946.

"Does Private Industry Threaten Freedom of Scientific Research?" A symposium by Hook et al. In **Science for Democracy**, edited by Jerome Nathanson, 54-108. New York: King's Crown Press, 1946.

"The Role of Science in Determination of Democratic Policy." A symposium by Hook et al. In **Science for Democracy**, edited by Jerome Nathanson, 109-70. New York: King's Crown Press, 1946.

"Fin du Mondisme: The Birth of a New World Mood in Face of Atombomb." *New Leader* 29 (23 Feb. 1946): 8-9.
Reply by Henry Zolan, "Liberal Writers." Ibid. 29 (1 June 1946): 18.

"Toward Intellectual Teamwork: Notes on the Evolution of a Conference."

Commentary 1 (Feb. 1946): 81-85.

"What Is Philosophy?" Review of **Philosophy in American Education: Its Tasks and Opportunities,** by Brand Blanshard, Curt J. Ducasse, Charles Van Hendel, Arthur E. Murphy, and Max C. Otto. *Nation* 162 (30 Mar. 1946): 375-77.

"Moral Values and/or Religion in Our Schools." *Progressive Education* 23 (May 1946): 256-57, 278-79.

"The Philosophic Scene: Scientific Method on the Defensive." *Commentary* 1 (June 1946): 85-90.

"Russia's Foreign Policy." Letter to the editor. *New York Times,* 17 Oct. 1946, 22.
>Response to letter by Arthur Upham Pope, ibid., 4 Oct. 1946, 22.
>Reply by Pope, "Reply on Russia." Ibid., 26 Oct. 1946, 16.
>Rejoinder by Hook, "Integrity of Criticism." Ibid., 2 Nov. 1946, 14.

"Oscar Lange--Polish Quisling." *New Leader* 29 (9 Nov. 1946): 9, 14.

"The 'Laws' of Dialectic." *Polemic* no. 6 (Nov.-Dec. 1946): 9-29.

"Synthesis or Eclecticism?" *Philosophy and Phenomenological Research* 7 (Dec. 1946): 214-25.
>Reply to Raphael Demos, "Philosophical Aspects of the Recent Harvard Report on Education." Ibid., 187-213.
>Reply by Demos, ibid., 264-92.
>Rejoinder by Hook, "From Question to Assertion: A Rejoinder to Professor Demos." Ibid. 7 (Mar. 1947): 439-45.
>Rejoinder by Harold Taylor, ibid., 446-52.

1947

Freedom and Experience: Essays Presented to Horace M. Kallen, edited by Sidney Hook and Milton R. Konvitz. Ithaca, N.Y.: Cornell University Press, 1947.
[Reviewed in *Annals of the American Academy of Political and Social Science* 257 (May 1948): 207-8 (Wilmon Henry Sheldon); *Ethics* 58 (Apr. 1948): 226-27 (Arthur Child); *Journal of Higher Education* 19 (Nov. 1948): 436 (Ordway Tead); *Journal of Philosophy* 45 (17 June 1948): 356-63 (Charles Frankel); *Modern Schoolman* 26 (Mar. 1949): 257-61 (James Collins); *New Leader* 31 (10 Jan. 1948): 11 (Ralph Gilbert Ross); *Philosophical Review* 57 (Nov. 1948): 613-19 (Roderick M.

Chisholm).]

"Intelligence and Evil in Human History." In **Freedom and Experience: Essays Presented to Horace M. Kallen**, edited by Sidney Hook and Milton R. Konvitz, 25-45. Ithaca, N.Y.: Cornell University Press, 1947; also printed in *Commentary* 3 (Mar. 1947): 210-21.
[Reprinted in **Pragmatism and the Tragic Sense of Life**, 1974.]

"The Future of Socialism." *Partisan Review* 14 (Jan.-Feb. 1947): 23-36.
Excerpts, "Totalitarian Liberalism." *Time* 49 (17 Feb. 1947): 28.
Reply by Don Calhoun, "Scapegoat for Liberals." *Pacifica Views* 4 (17 Feb. 1947): 3-4.

"Philosophy and the Police." Review of **Soviet Philosophy: A Study of Theory and Practice**, by John Somerville. *Nation* 164 (15 Feb. 1947): 188-89.
Reply by Somerville, ibid. 164 (10 May 1947): 554.
Response by Hook, ibid., 554-56.

"What Exactly Do We Mean by 'Democracy'?" *New York Times Magazine*, 16 Mar. 1947, 10, 48, 49.
Response by Martin Wolfson, "Liberty." Ibid., 6 Apr. 1947, 26.
Response by J. B. S. Halper, "Duality." Ibid.
Response by G. F. Ramirez, "Inherent." Ibid., 26, 28.

"An Integrated Synthesis." Contribution to A Symposium--III: Ideas for a New Party. *Antioch Review* 7 (June 1947): 305.

"An Unanswered Letter to The American Jewish Congress." *New Leader* 30 (5 July 1947): 14.

"Mr. Fly's Web of Confusions: A Problem of Contemporary Liberalism." *New Leader* 30 (18 Oct. 1947): 8, 9, 15.
Reply by James Lawrence Fly, "On the Befuddlement of Sidney Hook." Ibid. 30 (22 Nov. 1947): 8.
Rejoinder by Hook, "Mr. Fly Entangles Himself More Deeply." Ibid., 9, 15.
Comment by Hook, "Light on a Moot Point." Ibid. 30 (29 Nov. 1947): 14.
Comment by Judge Gordon Farley, "In Support of Sidney Hook." Ibid. 31 (10 Jan. 1948): 14.

"Is the U.S. a Republic or Democracy?" *New York Times Magazine*, 19 Oct. 1947, 17, 49, 50, 51.
Response by Hugh Diekman, "Self-Rule." Ibid., 9 Nov. 1947, 2.
Response by James T. Byrnes, "Ideas." Ibid.

Response by Murray Katz, "Both." Ibid., 23 Nov. 1947, 2.

"The U.S.S.R. Views American Philosophy." *Modern Review* 1 (Nov. 1947): 649-53. [Foreword to M. Dynnik, "Contemporary Bourgeois Philosophy in the U.S." Ibid., 653-60.]

"The Source of Value." Review of **An Analysis of Knowledge and Valuation**, by Clarence I. Lewis. *New York Times Book Review*, 16 Nov. 1947, 16.

"Moral und Politik." *Amerikanische Rundschau* 3 (1947): 3-18.

Letter to the editor. *Philosophical Review* 56 (1947): 608-9.
    Reply to Henry M. Wriston's review of **Education for Modern Man**, 1946. Ibid., 88-90.

"Portrait . . . John Dewey." *American Scholar* 17 (Winter 1947-48): 105-10.
    Reply by Howard Selsam, ibid. 17 (Summer 1948): 361-63.
    Response by Hook, ibid., 502, 504.
    Comment by Samuel Howard Titus, ibid. 18 (Spring 1949): 252-53.

1948

"Meeting of Logic and the Arts." Review of **The Logic of the Sciences and the Humanities**, by F. S. C. Northrop. *New York Times*, 11 Jan. 1948, 7.

"On the Casting Out of Devils." Review of **The Steep Places**, by Norman Angell. *New York Times Book Review*, 25 Jan. 1948, 1, 33.

"The Communist Manifesto 100 Years After." *New York Times Magazine*, 1 Feb. 1948, 6, 36, 38.
    Response by Martin Wolfson, "Turned Tables." Ibid., 22 Feb. 1948, 4.

"On Historical Understanding." *Partisan Review* 15 (Feb. 1948): 231-39. [Reprinted in **Pragmatism and the Tragic Sense of Life**, 1974.]

"The State--Servile or Free?" *New Leader* 31 (13 Mar. 1948): 1, 12.

"Academic Freedom. Violations in Soviet Satellite States Not Protested, It Is Said." Letter to the editor. *New York Times*, 23 Mar. 1948, 24.

"Why Democracy Is Better." *Commentary* 5 (Mar. 1948): 195-204.

"Religion in the Schools." Letter by Hook, William H. Kilpatrick, Vivian T. Thayer, R. Lawrence Siegel, Horace M. Kallen, and Dale DeWitt. *New*

York Times, 15 Apr. 1958, 24.

"Literature of Disenchantment." Review of **Lost Illusion**, by Freda Utley. *New York Times Book Review*, 16 May 1948, 1, 25.

"Mr. Toynbee's City of God." Review of **Civilization on Trial**, by Arnold Joseph Toynbee. *Partisan Review* 15 (June 1948): 691-99.
   Replies by C. Roland Wagner and E. G. Gallagher, ibid. 15 (Aug. 1948): 940-41.
   Response by Hook, ibid., 941-42.
[Reprinted in **Philosophy and Public Policy**, 1980.]

Letter to the editor. *American Scholar* 17 (Summer 1948): 360-61.
   Reply to Vera Micheles Dean, "U.S. Foreign Policy in the Atomic Age." Ibid. 17 (Winter 1947-48): 81-85.
   Reply to Saul K. Padover, "The American Century." Ibid., 85-90.
   Comments by Dean and Padover, ibid., 90-92.

"Russia's Slave Labor." Letter to the editor, by Hook, Robert M. MacIver, and Arthur Schlesinger. *New York Times*, 2 Nov. 1948, 24.
   Reply to "Russia's Slave Labor." Editorial. Ibid., 18 Oct. 1948, 22.

"Drei Grundzüge westlichen Denkens." *Der Monat* 1 (Nov. 1948): 8-17.

"New Palestine Party. Visit of Menachem Begin and Aims of Political Movement Discussed." Letter to the editor, by Hook et al. *New York Times*, 4 Dec. 1948, 12.

1949

"Academic Freedom and Communism." In **The People Shall Judge**, vol. 2, Social Sciences Staff, 705-14. Chicago: University of Chicago Press, 1949.

"Nature and the Human Spirit." In **Proceedings of the Tenth International Congress of Philosophy**, 153-55. Amsterdam: North-Holland Publishing Co., 1949.

"A Systematic Philosophy, and Testament, by Mr. Russell." Review of **Human Knowledge: Its Scope and Limit**, by Bertrand Russell. *New York Times Book Review*, 2 Jan. 1949, 8.

"Should Communists Be Permitted to Teach?" *New York Times Magazine*, 27 Feb. 1949, 7, 22, 24, 26, 28, 29.
   Comment, "Violators & Sympathizers." *Time* 53 (7 Mar. 1949):

46, 49.
> Responses by Robert K. Carr, L. B. Anderson, G. B., Jules Katz, Norman Thomas, Walter R. Storey, Walter Graham, Leone Adelson, and Kai E. Nielsen. *New York Times Magazine*, 13 Mar. 1949, 2, 4.
> Response by William Volk, "Communists as Teachers." Ibid., 20 Mar. 1949, 10.
> Response by Alexander Meiklejohn, "Should Communists Be Allowed to Teach?" Ibid., 27 Mar. 1949, 10, 64-66.
> Replies by Herman Wiener, Donald Montgomery, J. M. Russakoff, Lambert Fairchild, Naomi Barko, Joyce Pomeroy, Harold Affros, and Morton I. Moskowitz, ibid., 10 Apr. 1949, 2, 4.

"Communism and the Intellectuals." *American Mercury* 68 (Feb. 1949): 133-44.
> Letter by Howard Berger, "Communism and the Intellectuals." Ibid. 68 (May 1949): 635.

"Die Zukunft der demokratischen Linken." *Der Monat* 1 (Feb. 1949): 13-17.

"Geneticist's Dismissal Weighed." *New York Times*, 7 Mar. 1949, 20.
> Response to "Oregon Teacher Out As Lysenko Backer." Ibid., 24 Feb. 1949, 1.

"International Communism." *Dartmouth Alumni Magazine* 41 (Mar. 1949): 13-20.

"The Philosophy of Democracy as a Philosophy of History." *Philosophy and Phenomenological Research* 9 (Mar. 1949): 576-87.

"On the Battlefield of Philosophy." *Partisan Review* 16 (Mar. 1949): 251-68.

"Stand of the Liberals. Co-Chairmen of Group State Their Views on Cultural Conference." Letter to the editor by Hook and George S. Counts. *New York Times*, 13 Apr. 1949, 28.

"The Fellow-Traveler: A Study in Psychology." *New York Times Magazine*, 17 Apr. 1949, 9, 20, 21, 22, 23.
> Responses by M. J. Davis and David L. Weissman, ibid., 1 May 1949, 2.

[Reprinted in **Political Power and Personal Freedom**, 1959.]

"Dr. Hook Protests." Letter to the editor. *Nation* 168 (30 Apr. 1949): 511.
> Reply to Freda Kirchwey, "Battle of the Waldorf." Ibid. 168 (2 Apr.

1949): 377-78.
>Reply by Kirchwey, ibid. 168 (30 Apr. 1949): 511-13.

"Reflections on the Jewish Question." Review of **Anti-Semite and Jew,** by Jean-Paul Sartre. *Partisan Review* 16 (May 1949): 463-82.

"Science, Freedom and Peace." *New Leader* 32 (25 June 1949): 6.

"A Gallant American Rebel." Review of **The Bending Cross: A Biography of Eugene Victor Debs,** by Ray Ginger. *New York Times Book Review,* 17 July 1949, 7.

"Report on the International Day Against Dictatorship and War." *Partisan Review* 16 (July 1949): 722-32.

"What Shall We Do about Communist Teachers?" *Saturday Evening Post* 322 (10 Sept. 1949): 33, 164-67.
>Comment, "The Campus Communists." Ibid., 168.
[Reprinted in **Heresy, Yes--Conspiracy, No,** 1953.]

"The Literature of Political Disillusionment." *American Association of University Professors Bulletin* 35 (Autumn 1949): 450-67.

"John Dewey at Ninety: The Man and His Philosophy." *New Leader* 32 (22 Oct. 1949): S3, S8.

"Academic Integrity and Academic Freedom: How to Deal with the Fellow-Travelling Professor." *Commentary* 8 (Oct. 1949): 329-39.
>Reply by Charles A. Baylis, ibid. 8 (Nov. 1949): 500.
>Replies by Helen M. Lynd and Arthur E. Murphy, ibid. 8 (Dec. 1949): 594-98.
>Response by Hook, ibid., 598-601.
>Reply by Harold Taylor, ibid. 9 (Mar. 1950): 285-86.
[Reprinted in **Heresy, Yes--Conspiracy, No,** 1953.]

"Soviet Party Philosophy." *New York Times,* 18 Nov. 1949, 28.

"Academic Freedom: Academic Confusions." *Journal of Higher Education* 20 (Nov. 1949): 422-25.
>Response to Quincy Wright, "The Citizen's Stake in Academic Freedom." Ibid. 20 (Oct. 1949): 339-45; Harold W. Stoke, "Freedom Is Not Academic." Ibid., 346-49; John K. Ryan, "Truth and Freedom." Ibid., 349-52; Constance Warren, "Academic Freedom." Ibid., 353-54, 392.

"Comment." *Politics* 6 (Winter 1949): 35-36.

Reply to Cuthbert Daniel and Arthur M. Squires, "A First Step
Toward World Disarmament." Ibid., 28-34.
Reply by Daniel and Squires, ibid., 36.
Rejoinder by Hook, ibid.

1950

John Dewey: Philosopher of Science and Freedom, edited by Sidney Hook.
New York: Dial Press, 1950; New York: Barnes and Noble, 1967.
[Reviewed in *Booklist* 46 (15 June 1950): 310; *Choice* 4 (Oct. 1967): 852;
Ethics 61 (Oct. 1950): 89 (Alan Gewirth); *Humanist* 10 (Oct. 1950): 223
(Rubin Gotesky); *Journal of Philosophy* 48 (15 Mar. 1951): 192-95
(Harold Atkins Larrabee); *Journal of Symbolic Logic* 16 (Sept. 1951):
209 (Carl G. Hempel); *Modern Schoolman* 47 (Nov. 1969): 132-33 (Ken-
neth L. Becker); *New Leader* 33 (29 July 1950): 22 (Ordway Tead); *New
York Times Book Review*, 23 Apr. 1950, 6 (Thomas Vernor Smith); *San
Francisco Chronicle*, 6 Aug. 1950, 18 (R. H. U.); *Saturday Review* 33 (19
Aug. 1950): 35 (Robert Bierstedt); *Thought* 26 (Summer 1951): 288-91
(James Collins); *Western Humanities Review* 4 (Autumn 1950): 349-51
(Francis M. Myers).]

"Preface" and "The Desirable and Emotive in Dewey's Ethics." In **John
Dewey: Philosopher of Science and Freedom**, edited by Sidney Hook, v-
vi, 194-216. New York: Dial Press, 1950.
[Reprinted in **The Quest for Being**, 1961.]

"John Dewey and His Critics." In **Pragmatism and American Culture**,
edited by Gail Kennedy, 92-94. Boston: D. C. Heath and Co., 1950.

"The Place of John Dewey in Modern Thought." In **Philosophic Thought
in France and the United States**, edited by Marvin Farber, 483-503.
Buffalo: University of Buffalo Press, 1950.

Contribution in **Religion and the Intellectuals**. A symposium with John
Dewey, Hook et al. New York: Partisan Review, 1950.

"Democracy--Minus the Rhetoric." Review of **The Ramparts We Guard**, by
R. M. MacIver. *New York Times Book Review*, 26 Feb. 1950, 3, 31.

"Religion and the Intellectuals." *Partisan Review* 17 (Mar. 1950): 225-32.
Reply by Ernest van den Haag, ibid. 17 (July-Aug. 1950): 607-12.
Rejoinder by Hook, ibid., 612-16.
[Reprinted in **The Quest for Being**, 1961.]

"The Scientist in Politics." *New York Times Magazine*, 9 Apr. 1950, 10, 25,

27, 28, 30.
    Corrections by Hook, ibid., 23 Apr. 1950, 4.
    Reply by Editor, "Scientists' Views." Ibid., 30 Apr. 1950, 6.

"Communists in the Colleges." *New Leader* 33 (6 May 1950): 16-18.

"Lenin--oder Die Rolle des Einzelnen." *Der Monat* 2 (May 1950): 174-89.

"Heresy, Yes--But Conspiracy, No." *New York Times Magazine*, 9 July 1950, 12, 38-39.
    Reply by Edward Holton James, "Men of Concord." Ibid., 23 July 1950, 4.
    Response by Editor, ibid.
    Reply by J. M. Martinez, "Tag." Ibid., 30 July 1950, 2.
    Reply by John L. Childs, "Defending Rights." Ibid.
    Reply by George Garfield, "One World War." Ibid.
[Reprinted in **Heresy, Yes--Conspiracy, No**, 1953.]

"The Berlin Congress." Letter to the editor. *Manchester Guardian Weekly*, 7 Sept. 1950, 10.
    Reply to H. R. Trevor-Roper, "The Berlin 'Congress for Cultural Freedom.'" Ibid., 20 July 1950, 10.

"Past and Present of the Case That Shook the Nation." Review of **A Generation on Trial: U.S.A. v. Alger Hiss**, by Alistair Cooke. *New York Times Book Review*, 24 Sept. 1950, 7.

Review of **Out of My Later Years**, by Albert Einstein. *Annals of the American Academy of Political and Social Science* 271 (Sept. 1950): 201-3.

"The Berlin Congress for Cultural Freedom." *Partisan Review* 17 (Sept.-Oct. 1950): 715-22.

"The University of California and the Non-Communist Oath." Review of **The Year of the Oath**, by George R. Stewart et al. *New York Times Book Review*, 1 Oct. 1950, 6.
    Responses by Matthew Held, Richard E. Richman et al., ibid., 19 Nov. 1953, 43.
    Reply by Hook, ibid.

"Encounter in Berlin." *New Leader* 33 (14 Oct. 1950): 16-19.

"How to Stop Russia Without War." Review of **The Choice**, by Boris Shub. *New York Post*, 22 Oct. 1950, M16.

"Why They Switch Loyalties." *New York Times Magazine*, 26 Nov. 1950, 12,

26, 28, 30.

"U.N. Stand on Korea: Significance Stressed as Affirmation of Will to
Resist Communism." Letter to the editor. *New York Times*, 15 Dec.
1950, 30.
  Reply to Ralph Barton Perry, "Catastrophe of War." Ibid., 6 Dec.
  1950, 32.

1951

"Bertrand Russell's Philosophy of History." In **The Philosophy of Bertrand
Russell**, edited by Paul A. Schilpp, 645-78. New York: Tudor Publishing
Co., 1951.

"General Education: Its Nature and Purposes. Part II." In **General Education in Transition**, edited by Horace T. Morse, 68-82. Minneapolis:
University of Minnesota Press, 1951.

"Nature and the Human Spirit." In **Freedom and Reason**, edited by Salo
W. Baron, Ernest Nagel, and Koppel S. Pinson, 142-56. Glencoe, Ill.:
Free Press, 1951.
[Reprinted in **The Quest for Being**, 1961.]

"The Danger of Authoritarian Attitudes in Teaching Today." *School and
Society* 73 (20 Jan. 1951): 33-39.
[Abridged in *Socialist Call*, 26 Jan. 1951, 3, 5.]
[Reprinted in **Heresy, Yes--Conspiracy, No**, 1953.]

"Prof. Hook and the Loyalty Oaths." *Socialist Call*, 26 Jan. 1951, 3.
  Reply to Seymour Martin Lipset, "The Year of Many Loyalty Oaths
  at the University of California." Ibid., 12 Jan. 1951, 7-8.

"Coverage of Rousset Trial." Letter to the editor on slave labor in the
Soviet Union, by Hook et al. *New York Times*, 15 Feb. 1951, 30.

"To Counter the Big Lie--A Basic Strategy." *New York Times Magazine*, 11
Mar. 1951, 9, 59, 60, 61, 62, 63, 64.

"A Case Study in Anti-Secularism." Review of **The Moral Life and the
Ethical Life**, by Eliseo Vivas. *Partisan Review* 18 (18 Mar. 1951): 232-45.
[Reprinted in **Pragmatism and the Tragic Sense of Life**, 1974.]

"Liberty, Society and Mr. Santayana." Review of **Dominations and Powers**,
by George Santayana. *New York Times Book Review*, 6 May 1951, 1,
20.

"Academic Freedom: Integrity of American Scholars and Teachers
Affirmed." Letter to the editor. *New York Times*, 27 May 1951, 8.
Reply to "Freedom in the Colleges." Ibid., 11 May 1951, 26.

"Interpreting the Madison Incident." Letter to the editor. *New York Times*,
21 Aug. 1951, 26.
Reply by James M. Tyler, "Signing Petitions." Ibid., 29 Aug. 1951,
24.
Response by Hook, "Why Petitions Are Rejected." Ibid., 3 Sept.
1951, 12.

"The Dangers in 'Cultural Vigilantism.'" *New York Times Magazine*, 30
Sept. 1951, 9, 44, 46, 47.
Reply by Justin Wroe Nixon, "Vigilantism." Ibid., 7 Oct. 1951, 6.
Reply by Rose A. McGrath, "Absolute Truth." Ibid., 14 Oct. 1951, 4.
Reply by Mervin Ross, "Undue Optimism." Ibid.
Reply to McGrath by Conrad P. Homberger, "Truth." Ibid., 21 Oct.
1951, 5-6.
Reply to Homberger by Arnold B. Levinson, "Un-Platonic." Ibid., 4
Nov. 1951, 4.
Reply to Homberger by McGrath, "Pilgrim Fathers." Ibid., 11 Nov.
1951, 6.
Response by Homberger, "Plato vs. Dewey." Ibid., 18 Nov. 1951, 6.
[Reprinted in **Heresy, Yes--Conspiracy, No, 1953.**]

"Bread, Freedom, and Businessmen." *Fortune* 44 (Sept. 1951): 117, 176-88.
[Reprinted in **Political Power and Personal Freedom, 1959.**]

"The Use and Abuse of Words." Review of **Democracy in a World of Ten-
sions**, edited by Richard McKeon. *New Leader* 34 (15 Oct. 1951): 20-21.

"Russia by Moonshine, Part 1." *New Leader* 34 (12 Nov. 1951): 15-18.
"Part 2." Ibid. 34 (19 Nov. 1951): 12-14.
Replies by Gleb Struve and Jay W. Jensen, ibid. 34 (26 Nov. 1951):
28-29.
Reply by Henry C. Wolfe, ibid. 34 (17 Dec. 1951): 28.
Reply by T. Kobzey, ibid. 34 (24 Dec. 1951): 27-28.

1952

Democracy and Desegregation. New York: Tamiment Institute, 1952.

"The Role of Intelligence in Our Moral Awakening." A symposium by
Hook et al. In **Needed: A Moral Awakening in America**, edited by Harry
W. Laidler, 14-16. New York: League for Industrial Democracy, 1952.

"Academic Freedom and Its Values for Higher Education." In **Current Issues in Higher Education 1952,** by the National Conference on Higher Education, 70-75. Washington, D.C.: Association for Higher Education, 1952.

"Atheism." In **Collier's Encyclopedia**, vol. 2, 418. New York: P. F. Collier and Son, 1952.

"The Philosophical Basis of Marxian Socialism in the United States." In **Socialism and American Life**, vol. 1, edited by Donald Drew Egbert and Stow Persons, 427-51. Princeton, N.J.: Princeton University Press, 1952.

"Kann man die Freiheit essen?" *Der Monat* 4 (Jan. 1952): 339-44.

"Perennial and Temporal Goals in Education." *Journal of Higher Education* 23 (Jan. 1952): 1-12.
> Comments on Harold Benjamin and Robert M. Hutchins debate, "Education--What and How?" Ibid., 27-39.

"Mindless Empiricism." *Journal of Philosophy* 49 (14 Feb. 1952): 89-100.
> Reply to Victor Lowe, "A Resurgence of 'Vicious Intellectualism.'" Ibid. 48 (5 July 1951): 435-47.
> Reply by Lowe, "In Defense of Individualistic Empiricism: A Reply to Messrs. Lovejoy and Hook." Ibid., 100-111.
> Rejoinder by Arthur O. Lovejoy, "Rejoinder to Mr. Lowe." Ibid., 111-12.
> Rejoinder by Hook, "Not Mindful Enough." Ibid., 112-21.

"Cultural Freedom and Starving Men: A Case for Democracy." *Bharat Jyoti*, 16 Mar. 1952, 6.

"Degrees of Soviet Scholars." Letter to the editor. *New York Times*, 28 Apr. 1952, 18.

"The Faiths of Whittaker Chambers." Review of **Witness**, by Whittaker Chambers. *New York Times Book Review*, 25 May 1952, 1, 34-35.
> Letters by Herman F. Reissig et al., ibid., 22 June 1952, 17.
> Reply by Hook to Reissig, ibid.
> Comment by William S. Schlamm, *Freeman* 2 (30 June 1952): 665-66.
> Comment by Michael F. Moloney, "On Liberals Again." *America* 88 (11 Oct. 1952): 43-45.

"Russland in Mondenschein." *Der Monat* 4 (May 1952): 172-78.

"Academic Manners and Morals." *Journal of Higher Education* 23 (June 1952): 323-26, 342-43.

Response to Glenn Negley, "Liberty and Lawlessness." Ibid. 23 (Mar. 1952): 117-24.

"One Hit, One Miss." Review of **Communism, Democracy and Catholic Power**, by Paul Blanshard. *Twentieth Century* 152 (July 1952): 45-48.

"Our Country and Our Culture." A symposium by Hook et al. *Partisan Review* 19 (Sept. 1952): 569-74.
    Comment by John E. Connor, "Partisans." *Commonweal* 57 (13 Mar. 1953): 609-10.

"Some Memories of John Dewey." *Commentary* 14 (Sept. 1952): 245-53. [Reprinted in **Pragmatism and the Tragic Sense of Life**, 1974.]

"Letter to an English Friend." *New Leader* 35 (13 Oct. 1952): 16-18.
    Reply by Sidney Koretz, ibid. 35 (24 Nov. 1952): 28.
    Rejoinder by W. J. Smith and B. J. Green, "A Trans-Atlantic Dialogue." Ibid. 35 (8 Dec. 1952): 15-17.
    Reply by Hook, ibid., 17-20.
    Response by Green, ibid. 36 (26 Jan. 1953): 28-29.
    Reply by Hook, ibid. 36 (2 Feb. 1953): 27.

"The Fall of the Town of Usher." *New Leader* 35 (27 Oct. 1952): 16-19.
    Replies by Bela Fabian and Milton Hindus, ibid. 35 (24 Nov. 1952): 28.
    [Reprinted in **Political Power and Personal Freedom**, 1959.]

"John Dewey and Dr. Barnes." Letter to the editor. *Commentary* 14 (Nov. 1952): 504.
    Reply to Joseph Waldman, ibid., 503-4.

"Lattimore on the Moscow Trials." *New Leader* 35 (10 Nov. 1952): 16-19.
    Reply by J. C. Rich, ibid. 35 (1 Dec. 1952): 28.

"What Is 'Guilt by Association'?" *American Mercury* 75 (Nov. 1952): 37-43.
    [Reprinted in **Heresy, Yes--Conspiracy, No**, 1953.]

"Mr. Schlesinger's Record." Letter to the editor. *American Mercury* 75 (Nov. 1952): 68-69.
    Reply to James Burnham, "The Case against Adlai Stevenson." Ibid. 75 (Oct. 1952): 11-19.
    Reply by Burnham, ibid. 75 (Nov. 1952): 69.

"The Job of the Teacher in Days of Crisis." *New York Times Magazine*, 14 Dec. 1952, 9, 62, 63, 65.

1953

Heresy, Yes--Conspiracy, No. New York: John Day Co., 1953; New York: American Committee for Cultural Freedom, 1952.
[Reviewed in *America* 89 (6 June 1953): 282 (M. D. Reagan); *American Mercury* 77 (Aug. 1953): 143 (Frank Meyer); *Booklist* 49 (15 June 1953): 334; *Books on Trial* 11 (June 1953): 343 (Frank X. Steggert); *Chicago Sunday Tribune Magazine of Books*, 31 May 1953, 2 (Alfred C. Ames); *Christian Science Monitor*, 11 Sept. 1953, 9 (Saville R. Davis); *Commentary* 16 (July 1953): 86-88 (Robert E. Fitch); *Commonweal* 58 (15 May 1953): 155-56 (John Cogley); *Current History* 29 (Sept. 1955): 190-95 (David Denker); *Food for Thought* 14 (Nov. 1953): 8-10 (Harriet Rouillard); *Foreign Affairs* 31 (July 1953): 677-78 (Henry L. Roberts); *Fourth International* 14 (May-June 1953): 78-80 (Tom Milton); *Freeman* 3 (18 May 1953): 600-601 (Max Eastman); *Journal of Higher Education* 25 (Mar. 1954): 166-67 (A. Cornelius Benjamin); *Library Journal* 78 (1 June 1953): 992 (James Heslin); *Nation* 176 (6 June 1953): 484-85 (John W. Ward); *New Leader* 36 (8 June 1953): 21-22 (Ordway Tead); *New Republic* 128 (15 June 1953): 20 (Henry Bamford Parkes); *New York Herald Tribune Book Review*, 10 May 1953, 7 (August Heckscher); *New York Times Book Review*, 10 May 1953, 3 (Everett N. Case); *Saturday Review* 36 (13 June 1953): 13-14 (Arthur M. Schlesinger, Jr.); ibid. 36 (20 June 1953): 13, 38 (John K. Sherman); *Teachers College Record* 55 (Jan. 1954): 223-24 (James Marshall); *Thought* 28 (Winter 1953-54): 528-46 (Charles Donahue); *United Nations World* 7 (June 1953): 61-62 (George N. Shuster); *U.S. Quarterly Book Review* 9 (Sept. 1953): 328-29; *Virginia Law Review* 39 (Dec. 1953): 1136-39; *Yale Law Journal* 63 (Nov. 1953): 132-37 (Mark DeWolfe Howe).]

"The Ethics of Academic Freedom." In **Academic Freedom, Logic, and Religion,** edited by Morton G. White, 19-37. Symposium with George Boas. Philadelphia: University of Pennsylvania Press, 1953.

"The Quest for 'Being.'" In **Proceedings of the XIth International Congress of Philosophy, Brussels, 1953**, vol. xiv, 17-25. Amsterdam: North-Holland Publishing Co., 1953.

Letter to the editor on communism in the U.S. *Life* 34 (12 Jan. 1953): 7.
    Reply to editorial, "Heretics or Conspirators." Ibid. 33 (22 Dec. 1952): 14
    Comment by Bertrand N. Shaffer, ibid. 34 (12 Jan. 1953): 7.

"Soviet Anti-Semitism." Letter to the editor. *New York Times*, 30 Jan. 1953, 20.

"Does the Smith Act Threaten Our Liberties?" *Commentary* 15 (Jan.
   1953): 63-73.
      Responses by Adelaide Walker and Charles R. Walker III, and
         Albert Goldman, ibid. 15 (Mar. 1953): 305-8.
      Reply by Hook, ibid., 308-9.
      Reply by Victor Fox, ibid. 15 (Apr. 1953): 411.
   [Reprinted in **Heresy, Yes--Conspiracy, No**, 1953.]

"Education: Campuses Unlimited." *New York Times Magazine*, 1 Feb.
   1953, 70.

"Sidney Hook Replies to British Critic of United States Foreign Policy."
   New Leader 36 (2 Feb. 1953): 27.

"The Place of the Public School in American Life." Review of **Education
   and Liberty**, by James Bryant Conant. *New York Times Book Review*, 15
   Feb. 1953, 3.
      Responses by Walter R. Storey, Charles H. Connolly, T. Weakley,
         John K. Cunningham, and William L. Maier, ibid., 15 Mar. 1953,
         28.
      Reply by Hook, ibid.

"Should We Stress Armaments or Political Warfare?" Debate with Eliot
   Janeway. *New Leader* 36 (23 Feb. 1953): 17-19.

"Indoctrination and Academic Freedom." *New Leader* 36 (9 Mar. 1953):
   2-4.
      Replies by Mildred Berleman and William Withers, ibid. 36 (30 Mar.
         1953): 28.
      Replies by Charles Solomon and James Marshall, ibid. 36 (13 Apr.
         1953): 28-29.
      Response by Hook, ibid., 29.
      Reply by Milton R. Konvitz, "Justice and the Communist Teacher."
         Ibid. 36 (20 Apr. 1953): 16-19.
      Reply by A. Powell Davies, "Academic Freedom and the Communist
         Teacher." Ibid. 36 (11 May 1953): 15.
      Reply by Ernest van den Haag, "The Communist Teacher Can't Be
         Free." Ibid. 36 (25 May 1953): 12-14.
      Rejoinder by Solomon, ibid. 36 (1 June 1953): 28.
      Reply by Will Herberg, ibid., 28-29.
      Reply by Charles Cogen, ibid. 36 (22 June 1953): 20.

"Science et materialismé dialectique." In **Science et Liberté**, 22-30. Supplement to *Preuves*, no. 37, Mar. 1953.

"Freedom in American Culture." *New Leader* 36 (6 Apr. 1953): S3-S16.

Reply by High-School Teacher, ibid. 36 (20 Apr. 1953): 28.
Reply by Ralph M. Pons, ibid. 36 (27 Apr. 1953): 27.
Reply by John J. Donohue, ibid. 36 (1 June 1953): 28.
[Reprinted in **Heresy, Yes--Conspiracy, No**, 1953.]

"Can We Trust Our Teachers?" *Saturday Review* 36 (18 Apr. 1953): 11, 12,
45-47.
Replies by Gwynne Nettler, William T. Couch, and Stanley
Cooperman, ibid. 36 (23 May 1953): 21.

"Mr. McCarthy Criticized." *New York Times*, 8 May 1953, 24.
Reply by Frederic S. Allen, "McCarthy Seen Hurting Country."
Ibid., 22 May 1953, 26.

"The Words Came Easily." Review of **Harold Laski (1893-1950): A
Biographical Memoir**, by Kingsley Martin. *New York Times Book
Review*, 17 May 1953, 7, 33.
Response by Stanley Plastrik, "Laski and Communism." Ibid., 12
July 1953, 19.
Reply by Hook, ibid.

"The Party Line on Psychology." Review of **This Matter of Mind**, by Brian
H. Kirman. *New Leader* 36 (25 May 1953): 23-24.

"Freedom to Teach." Letter by Hook, George S. Counts, Paul R. Hays, and
Arthur O. Lovejoy. *New York Times*, 19 July 1953, 10.
Reply by Willford L. King, "Academic Freedom." Ibid., 26 July 1953,
6.
Reply by Lester G. Crocker, "Freedom of Thought." Ibid., 2 Aug.
1953, 6.
["In Defense of Academic Autonomy." Partial text of statement. *New
Leader* 36 (27 July 1953): 11.]

Letter to the editor. *New Leader* 36 (5 Oct. 1953): 27-29.
Reply to Broadus Mitchell, "Opposes Firing Teachers for Communist Membership." Ibid., 27.

"The Fifth Amendment--A Moral Issue." *New York Times Magazine*, 1
Nov. 1953, 9, 57, 59-60, 62, 64, 66.
Replies by Osmond K. Fraenkel, Leo J. Reiss, and Milton Ost, ibid.,
15 Nov. 1953, 6.

"The Quest for 'Being.'" *Journal of Philosophy* 50 (19 Nov. 1953): 709-31.
Reply by John Herman Randall, Jr., "On Being Rejected." Ibid. 50
(17 Dec. 1953): 797-805.
[Reprinted in **The Quest for Being**, 1961.]

1954

"Modern Education and Its Critics." In **American Association of Colleges Yearbook,** 139-60. Oneonta, N.Y.: American Association of Colleges, 1954.

"The Individual in a Totalitarian Society." In **The Contemporary Scene,** 1-18. Symposium by the Metropolitan Museum of Art, 28-30 Mar. 1952. New York: Metropolitan Museum of Art, 1954.

"The Ethics of Controversy." *New Leader* 37 (1 Feb. 1954): 12-14.
    Replies by Nathan D. Shapiro and Andrew Green, ibid. 37 (1 Mar. 1954): 29-30.
[Reprinted in **Philosophy and Public Policy,** 1980.]

"Symposium: Are Religious Dogmas Cognitive and Meaningful?" *Journal of Philosophy* 51 (4 Mar. 1954): 165-68.

"The Techniques of Controversy." Including discussion of **The Secret War for the A-Bomb,** by Medford Evans. *New Leader* 37 (8 Mar. 1954): 15-18.
    Reply by G. Wachsner, ibid. 37 (22 Mar. 1954): 29.
    Reply by A. J. Muste, ibid. 37 (5 Apr. 1954): 29.
    Response by Hook, ibid., 29-30.

"Articles of the Bolshevik Faith." Review of **A Study of Bolshevism,** by Nathan Leites. *New York Times Book Review,* 28 Mar. 1954, 10.

"Robert Hutchins Rides Again." *New Leader* 37 (19 Apr. 1954): 16-19.
    Comment by Katharine Taylor, ibid. 37 (17 May 1954): 29.

"Rigors of Heresy." Review of **The Test of Freedom,** by Norman Thomas. *Saturday Review* 37 (24 Apr. 1954): 16-17.

"Myths of Marx." Review of **Where We Came Out,** by Granville Hicks. *Saturday Review* 37 (15 May 1954): 11-12.

"Unpragmatic Liberalism." Review of **Freedom, Loyalty and Dissent,** by Henry Steele Commager. *New Republic* 130 (24 May 1954): 18-21.

"The Substance of Controversy: A Reply." *New Leader* 37 (24 May 1954): 18-19.
    Reply to Medford Evans, "The Substance of Controversy." Ibid., 16-18.
[See "The Techniques of Controversy," 8 Mar. 1954.]

"Uncommon Sense About Security and Freedom." *New Leader* 37 (21 June 1954): 8-10.

"Security and Freedom." *Confluence* 3 (June 1954): 155-71.
   [Reprinted in **Political Power and Personal Freedom**, 1959.]

"The Problem of the Ex-Communist." *New York Times Magazine*, 11 July 1954, 7, 24-27.
      Reply by Cornelius F. Kelly, Jr., "Skepticism." Ibid., 25 July 1954, 46.

"Should Our Schools Study Communism?" *New York Times Magazine*, 29 Aug. 1954, 9, 24, 26.
      Response by Gerald A. Rogovin, ibid., 12 Sept. 1954, 5.
      Correction by Hook, ibid.
      Response by J. Anthony Marcus, "Communism's Twin?" Ibid., 19 Sept. 1954, 4.
      Editor's comment, ibid.
      Response by Edward Hill, "On Teaching 'Communism' in Our Schools: Professor Hook Performs 'A Ritual of Silence.'" *Young Socialist Challenge*, 6 Sept. 1954, 1.
      Response by Howard Selsam, ibid., 26 Sept. 1954, 6.
      Reply by Hook, ibid., 10 Oct. 1954, 6.

"Why Some Sign Up." Review of **The Appeals of Communism**, by Gabriel A. Almond et al. *New York Times Book Review*, 19 Sept. 1954, 3, 28, 29.

"Sikkerhed og Frihed." *Det Danske Magasin* 2 (1954): 441-58.

1955

Dialectical Materialism and Scientific Method. Manchester, England: J. B. Foy and Co., 1955.

Marx and the Marxists: The Ambiguous Legacy. Princeton, N.J.: D. Van Nostrand Co., 1955.
   [Reviewed in *American Sociological Review* 21 (June 1956): 397-98 (Paul W. Massing); *Library Journal* 80 (15 Sept. 1955): 1904 (H. H. Bernt); *Review of Metaphysics* 10 (Sept. 1956): 177 (Richard G. Schmitt); *Review of Politics* 18 (Apr. 1956): 254-56 (Gerhart Niemeyer).]

Introduction to **The Logic of Moral Discourse**, by Paul Edwards, 13-16. Glencoe, Ill.: Free Press, 1955.

"Science and Dialectical Materialism." In **Science and Freedom**, proceed-

ings of a conference convened by the Congress for Cultural Freedom, Hamburg, 23-26 July 1953, 182-95. Boston: Beacon Press, 1955. See also Hook's contributions to discussions, ibid., 47-48, 114-15, 144-46, 263-64.
[Reprinted in **Political Power and Personal Freedom**, 1959.]

"Historical Determinism and Political Fiat in Soviet Communism." *Proceedings of the American Philosophical Society* 99 (Jan. 1955): 1-10.
[Reprinted in **Political Power and Personal Freedom**, 1959.]

"Fallacies in Our Thinking about Security." *New York Times Magazine*, 30 Jan. 1955, 15, 33, 35.

"A Question of Means and Ends in a World Threatened by Evil." Review of **Human Society in Ethics and Politics**, by Bertrand Russell. *New York Times Book Review*, 30 Jan. 1955, 3.

"On Security and Freedom." *Freedom and Union* 10 (Apr. 1955): 10-15.

"Marx in Limbo: An Imaginary Conversation." *New Leader* 38 (2 May 1955): 14-17.
Comment by Julius Gerber, ibid. 38 (23 May 1955): 29-30.
Comment by Irving Howe, *Dissent* 2 (Spring 1955): 285-86.
[Reprinted in **Political Power and Personal Freedom**, 1959.]

"Tyranny through the Ages." Review of **Why Dictators?** by George W. F. Hallgarten. *New Leader* 38 (6 June 1955): 18-19.
Reply by Hallgarten, ibid. 38 (7 Nov. 1955): 29-30.

"A Steady Light." Review of **John Dewey: His Contribution to the American Tradition**, edited by Irwin Edman. *New York Times Book Review*, 24 July 1955, 3, 20.

"The Grounds on Which Our Educators Stand." Review of **The Development of Academic Freedom in the United States**, by Richard Hofstadter and Walter P. Metzger, and **Academic Freedom in Our Time**, by Robert M. MacIver. *New York Times Book Review*, 30 Oct. 1955, 6, 28.
Responses by John M. Pickering, Lawrence M. Madigan, Robert Bierstedt, Clement C. Sullivan, and Harold Taylor, ibid., 27 Nov. 1955, 52.
Reply by Hook, ibid., 52-53.

"The Teaching and the Taught." Review of **Collectivism on the Campus**, by E. Merrill Root. *New York Times Book Review*, 6 Nov. 1955, 58.
Response by Root, ibid., 25 Dec. 1955, 12.
Reply by Hook, ibid.

Introduction to "Communism's Postwar Decade," by Simon Wolin. *New Leader* 38 (19 Dec. 1955): S2-S4; New York: Tamiment Institute, 1956.

1956

American Philosophers at Work, edited by Sidney Hook. New York:
Criterion Books, 1956.
[Reviewed in *Booklist* 53 (15 Jan. 1957): 236-37; *Commentary* 24 (Nov.
1957): 454-60 (Kathleen Nott); *Encounter* 8 (Apr. 1957): 78-80 (Stuart
Hampshire); *New Leader* 40 (1 Apr. 1957): 23-24 (Ralph Gilbert Ross);
New Republic 136 (17 June 1957): 16-18 (Robert E. Fitch); *New York
Herald Tribune Book Review*, 27 Jan. 1957, 12; *New York Times Book
Review*, 23 Dec. 1956, 3, 14 (Reinhold Niebuhr); *Personalist* 39 (Jan.
1958): 68-69 (W. H. Werkmeister); *Review of Metaphysics* 10 (June
1957): 726-27 (Charles Landesman); ibid. 11 (Dec. 1957): 279-82 (John
E. Smith); *Thought* 32 (Winter 1957-58): 620-21 (W. Norris Clarke).]

"Introduction" and "Naturalism and First Principles." In **American
Philosophers at Work**, edited by Sidney Hook, 9-13, 236-58.
[Reprinted in **The Quest for Being**, 1961.]

"The Ethics of Controversy Again." *New Leader* 39 (16 Jan. 1956): 16-18.
Analysis of exchange between Max Eastman and Robert M. MacIver,
ibid. 38 (5 Dec. 1955): 20-21.
Reply by Webster E. Cotton, "Liberalism." Ibid. 39 (12 Mar. 1956):
29.
[See "The Ethics of Controversy," 1 Feb. 1954.]

"Prophet of Man's Glory and Tragedy." Review of **Reinhold Niebuhr--His
Religious, Social and Political Thought**, edited by Charles W. Kegley
and Robert W. Bretall. *New York Times Book Review*, 29 Jan. 1956, 6, 7,
22.
[Reprinted in **Pragmatism and the Tragic Sense of Life**, 1974.]

"The Strategy of Truth." *New Leader* 39 (13 Feb. 1956): 21-24.
Reply to Milton R. Konvitz, "Are Teachers Afraid?" Ibid., 17-21.

"Six Fallacies of Robert Hutchins." *New Leader* 39 (19 Mar. 1956): 18-28.
Announcement, ibid. 39 (5 Mar. 1956): 2.
Responses, ibid. 39 (2 Apr. 1956): 28-29; ibid. 39 (9 Apr. 1956): 22;
ibid. 39 (16 Apr. 1956): 29; ibid. 39 (23 Apr. 1956): 28-29; ibid. 39
(14 May 1956): 29.
Replies by Hook, ibid. 39 (16 Apr. 1956): 29-30; ibid. 39 (23 Apr.
1956): 28-29.
Comment, "Hook vs. Hutchins." *America* 94 (31 Mar. 1956): 708.

"Exposing Soviet Purges." *New York Times*, 1 Apr. 1956, 8.

"Case of de Galindez." Letter by Hook et al. *New York Times*, 24 Apr. 1956, 30.

"Prospects for Cultural Freedom." *New Leader* 39 (7 May 1956): S5-S8.

"The AAUP and Academic Integrity." *New Leader* 39 (21 May 1956): 19-21.
> Response by Cormac Philip, ibid. 39 (4 June 1956): 29.
> Rejoinder by Hook, ibid., 29.
> Response by Ralph F. Fuchs, ibid. 39 (25 June 1956): 28-29.
> Rejoinder by Hook, ibid., 29-31.
> Responses by Pierre Aubeuf and Arthur O. Lovejoy, ibid. 39 (2 July 1956): 21-22.
> Response by William W. Edel, ibid. 39 (16 July 1956): 13.
> Response by Sam Lambert, ibid. 39 (13 Aug. 1956): 22.
[Reprinted in **Political Power and Personal Freedom**, 1959.]

"The Scope of Philosophy of Education." *Harvard Educational Review* 26 (Spring 1956): 145-48.
[Reprinted in **Education and the Taming of Power**, 1973.]

"Education and Creative Intelligence." *School and Society* 84 (7 July 1956): 3-8.
[Reprinted in **Education and the Taming of Power**, 1973.]

"Wanted, an Ethics of Employment for Our Time." Review of **Report on Blacklisting**, by John Cogley. *New York Times Book Review*, 22 July 1956, 6, 14.
> Responses by Clark Godfrey, Ruth Horowitz, A. J. Muste, Black-listed Anti-Communist Actor, and Irving Louis Horowitz, ibid., 19 Aug. 1956, 22.
> Reply by Hook, ibid.

"The Jurisdiction of Intelligence." *School and Society* 84 (4 Aug. 1956): 35-39.
[See "Education and Creative Intelligence," 7 July 1956.]

Comments on **The Fifth Amendment Today**, by Erwin N. Griswold. "Logic and the Fifth Amendment." *New Leader* 39 (1 Oct. 1956): 12-22; "Psychology and the Fifth Amendment." Ibid. 39 (8 Oct. 1956): 20-24; "Ethics and the Fifth Amendment." Ibid. 39 (15 Oct. 1956): 16-24; "Politics and the Fifth Amendment." Ibid. 39 (22 Oct. 1956): 16-23.
> Reply by Griswold, "The Individual and the Fifth Amendment." Ibid. 39 (29 Oct. 1956): 20-23.

Rejoinder by Hook, "Logic, History and Law: A Rejoinder to Dean
  Griswold." Ibid. 39 (5 Nov. 1956): 12-15.
Comment by Arthur W. Calhoun, ibid. 39 (29 Oct. 1956): 30.
[Reprinted in **Common Sense and the Fifth Amendment**, 1957.]

"Right to Equal Treatment." Letter to the editor. *New York Times*, 7 Nov.
  1956, 30.

"Sense and Salvation." Review of **The Outsider**, by Colin Wilson. *Commentary* 22 (Nov. 1956): 479-80, 82.

"Man as a Whole." Letter to the editor on school segregation. *Listener* 56
  (27 Dec. 1956): 1076-77.
    Reply to John U. Nef, "Man as a Whole." Ibid. 56 (29 Nov. 1956):
      875-76.
    Reply by Nef, "Man as a Whole." Ibid. 57 (7 Feb. 1957): 233, 235.

"Filosofien i den moderne verden." *Perspektiv* 4 (Dec. 1956): 28-30.

"A Joint Statement on a Matter of Importance." With Ralph F. Fuchs.
  American Association of University Professors Bulletin 42 (Dec. 1956):
  692-95.
[See "The AAUP and Academic Integrity," 21 May 1956.]

1957

Common Sense and the Fifth Amendment. New York: Criterion Books,
  1957.
  [Reviewed in *Bookmark* 16 (June 1957): 210; *Chicago Sunday Tribune
  Magazine of Books*, 19 May 1957, 3 (Willard Edwards); *Cleveland Open
  Shelf*, Nov. 1957, 20; *Commentary* 25 (Jan. 1958): 83-86 (Maurice J.
  Goldbloom); *Critic* 16 (Aug.-Sept. 1957): 16 (Albert H. Miller); *De Paul
  Law Review* 7 (Autumn-Winter 1957): 141-45 (Nathaniel L. Nathanson);
  Kirkus 25 (1 Mar. 1957): 203; *Library Journal* 82 (15 Apr. 1957): 1053
  (Louis Barron); *New Leader* 40 (10 June 1957): 22-23 (Carl A. Auer-
  bach); *New Yorker* 33 (11 May 1957): 163-64; *New York Herald Tribune
  Book Review*, 9 June 1957, 6 (William H. Edwards); *New York Times
  Book Review*, 26 May 1957, 3, 12 (John B. Oakes); *Saturday Review* 40
  (10 Aug. 1957): 32-33 (Harry Kalven, Jr.); *Stanford Law Review* 10 (July
  1958): 785-92 (Leon Lipson); *Time* 69 (27 May 1957): 111-12; *Villanova
  Law Review* 3 (Jan. 1958): 248-51 (William B. Ball); *Yale Review*, n.s. 47
  (Autumn 1957): 117-25 (Charles L. Black, Jr.).]

"Outlook for Philosophy." In **New Frontiers of Knowledge: A Symposium
  by Distinguished Writers, Notable Scholars and Public Figures**, edited

by M. B. Schnapper, 18-21. Washington, D.C.: Public Affairs Press, 1957.
[Reviewed in *Personalist* 40 (Summer, July 1959): 318 (J. W. Robb).]

"The Monolithic State." Review of **Totalitarian Dictatorship and Autocracy**, by Carl J. Friedrich and Zbigniew K. Brzezinski. *New York Times Book Review*, 20 Jan. 1957, 3, 36.

"Liberalism and the Law: Justice Frankfurter and Professor Chafee." *Commentary* 23 (Jan. 1957): 46-56.
    Response by C. Rajagopalachari, ibid. 23 (Apr. 1957): 380.
[Reprinted in **Political Power and Personal Freedom**, 1959.]

"From Opera Bouffe to Treason." Review of **The Roots of American Communism**, by Theodore Draper. *Saturday Review* 40 (16 Mar. 1957): 14-15.

"Abraham Lincoln, American Pragmatist." *New Leader* 40 (18 Mar. 1957): 16-18.
        Reply by Max Eastman, "Lincoln Was No Pragmatist." Ibid. 40 (23 Sept. 1957): 19-20.
        Response by Hook, "Marx, Dewey and Lincoln." Ibid. 40 (21 Oct. 1957): 16-18.
        Response by Bernard Herman and Martin Gardner, "Hook's Marx." Ibid. 40 (18 Nov. 1957): 28-29.
        Reply by Hook, "Pragmatism." Ibid. 40 (9 Dec. 1957): 29-30.
        Response by Eastman, "A Debate on Pragmatism: Marx, Dewey and Hook." Ibid. 41 (10 Feb. 1958): 16-18.
        Reply by Hook, "Marx, Dewey and Eastman." Ibid., 18-19.

"The Fifth Amendment: A Crucial Case." *New Leader* 40 (22 Apr. 1957): 18-20.

"Use of Fifth Amendment Discussed." *New York Times*, 10 May 1957, 26.
        Reply by Irving Mariash, ibid., 17 May 1957, 24.
        Response by Hook, "Limits of Immunity Grants." Ibid., 25 May 1957, 20.

"A Fateful Chapter of Our Times." Review of **In the Court of Public Opinion**, by Alger Hiss. *New York Times Book Review*, 12 May 1957, 1, 28, 29.

"Scientific Knowledge and Philosophical 'Knowledge.'" *Partisan Review* 24 (Spring 1957): 215-34.
[Reprinted in **The Quest for Being**, 1961.]

"The Atom and Human Wisdom." *New Leader* 40 (3 June 1957): 8-10.

"The Old Liberalism and the New Conservatism." *New Leader* 40 (8 July 1957): 7-10.

"The Affair Hiss." *Encounter* 9 (July 1957): 81-84.

"Moral Judgment and Historical Ambiguity." *Problems of Communism* 6 (July-Aug. 1957): 47-50; *New Leader* 40 (19 Aug. 1957): 16-19.

"Socialism and Liberation." *Partisan Review* 24 (Fall 1957): 497-518.
[Reprinted in **Political Power and Personal Freedom**, 1959.]
Condensed as "The Import of Ideological Diversity." *Problems of Communism* 6 (Nov.-Dec. 1957): 11-18.
[Reprinted in **Revolution, Reform, and Social Justice**, 1975.]

"The Red Lodestar." Review of **The Opium of the Intellectuals**, by Raymond Aron. *Saturday Review* 40 (23 Nov. 1957): 18-20.

"Justice Black's Illogic." *New Leader* 40 (2 Dec. 1957): 17-20.

1958

Determinism and Freedom in the Age of Modern Science, edited by Sidney Hook. First Symposium, New York University Institute of Philosophy, 9-10 Feb. 1957. New York: New York University Press, 1958.
[Reviewed in *Annals of the American Academy of Political and Social Science* 320 (Nov. 1958): 177-78 (Rubin Gotesky); *Heythrop Journal* 5 (Jan. 1964): 116-17 (C. M. S.); *International Philosophical Quarterly* 1 (Sept. 1961): 516-32 (Joseph F. Donceel); *Journal of Philosophy* 56 (9 Apr. 1959): 369-73 (Arthur C. Danto); *Library Journal* 83 (1 Apr. 1958): 1081 (Robert W. Henderson); *Mind* 69 (Jan. 1960): 110-12 (Norman Brown); *Modern Schoolman* 37 (Mar. 1960): 246-47 (Joseph F. Collins); *New York Times Book Review*, 16 Nov. 1958, 47 (Charles Frankel); *Philosophical Quarterly* 10 (July 1960): 282-83 (H. J. N. Horsburgh); *Ratio* 5 (Dec. 1963): 213-23 (D. F. Pears); *Review of Metaphysics* 12 (Sept. 1958): 145 (J. F. D.); *Review of Politics* 23 (Jan. 1961): 96-97 (Karl Kreilkamp); *Revue philosophique de Louvain* 60 (Nov. 1962): 622-37 (Gérard Deledalle).]

"Preface" and "Necessity, Indeterminism, and Sentimentalism." In **Determinism and Freedom in the Age of Modern Science**, edited by Sidney Hook, xiii-xv, 167-80. New York: New York University Press, 1958.

"The Missing Link in American Science." *New Leader* 41 (6 Jan. 1958): 16-19; *Freedom and Union* 13 (June 1958): 19.
>   Replies by Susan Bodan, Sol Feinstone, Edward J. Rozek, E. Burton, and A. M. Wallach, ibid. 41 (3 Feb. 1958): 28-29.

"Befreiung durch Evolution." *Der Monat* 10 (Feb. 1958): 10-25.

"A Foreign Policy for Survival." *New Leader* 41 (7 Apr. 1958): 8-12.
>   Response by Bertrand Russell, "World Communism and Nuclear War." Ibid. 41 (26 May 1958): 9-10.
>   Reply by Hook, "A Free Man's Choice." Ibid., 10-12.
>   Response by David Zaslavsky, "Grotesque Controversy." Ibid. 41 (18-25 Aug. 1958): 13-14.
> [Reprinted in **Political Power and Personal Freedom**, 1959.]

"Democracy and Desegregation." *New Leader* 41 (21 Apr. 1958): Sec. 2, 3-19.
>   Response by Hannah Arendt, "Reflections on Little Rock." *Dissent* 6 (Winter 1959): 45-56.
>   Reply by Hook, "Hannah Arendt's Reflections." Ibid. 6 (Spring 1959): 203.
>   Response by Arendt, ibid., 203-4.
> [Reprinted in **Political Power and Personal Freedom**, 1959.]

"A Look at the Evidence in a Famous Case." Review of **The Unfinished Story of Alger Hiss**, by Fred J. Cook. *New York Times Book Review*, 4 May 1958, 4, 20.
>   Responses by William M. Kunstler, Erica and Bernard Landis, and Joseph N. Ulman, Jr., ibid., 1 June 1958, 14.

"Bureaucrats Are Human." *Saturday Review* 41 (17 May 1958): 12-14, 41.
> [Reprinted in **Revolution, Reform, and Social Justice**, 1975.]

"Moral Freedom in a Determined World." *Commentary* 25 (May 1958): 431-43.
> [Reprinted in **The Quest for Being**, 1961.]

"Bertrand Russell Retreats." *New Leader* 41 (7-14 July 1958): 25-28.
>   Response to Bertrand Russell, "Freedom to Survive." Ibid., 23-25.
> [See "A Foreign Policy for Survival," 7 Apr. 1958.]
> [Reprinted in **Political Power and Personal Freedom**, 1959.]

"Die letzte Entscheidung: Ein Streitgespräch über die Atombombe." *Der Monat* 10 (July 1958): 11-16.

Reply by Bertrand Russell, "Keine Despotie währt ewig." Ibid., 16-18.

Response by Hook, "Grenzen der Nachgiebigkeit." Ibid., 18-21.

Response by Russell, "Die Freiheit zu überleben." Ibid. 10 (Sept. 1958): 81-84.

Reply by Hook, "Mehr als zu überleben." Ibid., 84-89.

"Socialism and Democracy." *New Leader* 41 (3 Nov. 1958): 17-18.

"Education in Japan." *New Leader* 41 (24 Nov. 1958): 8-11.

1959

John Dewey: His Philosophy of Education and Its Critics. New York: Tamiment Institute, 1959.
[Reviewed in *National Review* 8 (30 Jan. 1960): 79-80 (Thomas Molnar).]

Political Power and Personal Freedom: Critical Studies in Democracy, Communism, and Civil Rights. New York: Criterion Books, 1959.
[Collier Macmillan paperback, 1962.]
[Reviewed in *American Political Science Review* 53 (Dec. 1959): 1140-41 (Morton Auerbach); *Annals of the American Academy of Political and Social Science* 327 (Jan. 1960): 140 (Rubin Gotesky); *Booklist* 56 (1 Sept. 1959): 18; *Chicago Sunday Tribune Magazine of Books*, 12 July 1959, 6 (Willard Edwards); *Christian Science Monitor*, 25 June 1959, 11 (Earl W. Foell); *Foreign Affairs* 38 (Oct. 1959): 147-48 (Henry L. Roberts); *Kirkus* 27 (1 June 1959): 390-91; *New Scholasticism* 34 (July 1960): 382-84 (Eugene J. McCarthy); *New York Herald Tribune Book Review*, 8 Nov. 1959, 14 (Robert K. Carr); *New York Times Book Review*, 13 Sept. 1959, 20 (Ernest van den Haag); *Political Science Quarterly* 75 (Mar. 1960): 111-13 (Robert Lekachman); *Saturday Review* 42 (5 Sept. 1959): 18-19 (Norman Thomas); *Yale Review*, n.s. 49 (Autumn 1959): 139-41 (William Miller).]

Psychoanalysis, Scientific Method, and Philosophy, edited by Sidney Hook. Second Symposium, New York University Institute of Philosophy, 28-29 Mar. 1958. New York: New York University Press, 1959.
[Reviewed in *American Sociological Review* 24 (Dec. 1959): 927-28 (Richard T. LaPiere); *Antioch Review* 20 (Fall 1960): 391-96 (Virginia Held); *British Journal for the Philosophy of Science* 13 (May 1962): 56-65 (Max Teichmann); *Christian Century* 76 (4 Nov. 1959): 1283; *Ethics* 71 (Oct. 1960): 56-58 (Mary Mothersill); *Journalism Quarterly* 36 (Summer 1959): 360 (Edgar and Lois Crane); *Library Journal* 84 (1 June 1959):

1901 (George Adelman); *New Scholasticism* 34 (Apr. 1960): 258-62
(Antos C. Rancurello); *Personalist* 41 (July 1960): 382-83 (William H.
Werkmeister); *Philosophical Review* 70 (Jan. 1961): 123-25 (Sydney
Shoemaker); *Philosophy and Phenomenological Research* 20 (June 1960):
550-52 (Lewis S. Feuer); *Saturday Review* 42 (11 July 1959): 30-31 (John
Sullivan); ibid. 43 (22 Oct. 1960): 33; *Thomist* 24 (Jan. 1961): 109-11
(Rudolf Allers).]

"Introduction" and "Science and Mythology in Psychoanalysis." In
Psychoanalysis, Scientific Method, and Philosophy, edited by
Sidney Hook, xi-xiii, 212-24. New York: New York University Press,
1959.

"John Dewey, 1859-1952." In **Philosophy in the Mid-Century**, vol. 4, edited
by Raymond Klibansky, 210-14. International Institute of Philosophy,
1958-1959. Florence: La Nuova Italia, 1959.

"Proletariat." In **Encyclopaedia Britannica**, 14th ed., 576. Chicago:
Encyclopaedia Britannica, 1959.

"The Philosophical Bases of Education." In **Proceedings of the Summer
Conference**, Western Washington College of Education, 3-15.
Bellingham: Western Washington College of Education, 1959.
    Comment by Halldor Karason, ibid., 16-18.
    Comment by Neville Scarfe, ibid., 19-21.

"The Psychological Bases of Education." In **Proceedings of the Summer
Conference**, Western Washington College of Education, 22-33.
Bellingham: Western Washington College of Education, 1959.
    Comment by Henry Adams, ibid., 34-36.
    Comment by Maurice Freehill, ibid., 37-38.

"The Social Bases of Education." In **Proceedings of the Summer
Conference**, Western Washington College of Education, 39-50.
Bellingham: Western Washington College of Education, 1959.
    Comment by A. LeRoy Bennett, ibid., 51-53.
    Comment by Herbert C. Taylor, Jr., ibid., 54-57.

"What Is Education?" With George N. Shuster and Panel. In **Education in
the Age of Science**, edited by Brand Blanshard, 1-52. New York: Basic
Books, 1959.
[Condensed and reprinted in *Science Teacher* 26 (Nov. 1959): 462-67,
516-21.]

"Conscience and Consciousness in Japan." *Commentary* 27 (Jan. 1959):

59-66.

"Which Way Japan?" *New Leader* 42 (9 Feb. 1959): 3-7.

"The Impact of Ideas." Review of **Consciousness and Society: The Reorientation of European Social Thought, 1890-1930**, by H. Stuart Hughes. *New York Times Book Review*, 29 Mar. 1959, 22.

"The Philosophy of Reading." *Proceedings of the 41st and 42nd Annual University of Delaware School of Education Conferences* 8 (Mar. 1959): 20-34.

"Grim Report: Asia in Transition." *New York Times Magazine*, 5 Apr. 1959, 11, 104, 106, 108.
    Reply by Richard A. Long, "Open Wound." Ibid., 19 Apr. 1959, 4.

"Man and Nature: Some Questions for Mr. Mitin." *Journal of Philosophy* 56 (23 Apr. 1959): 408-16.

"J. H. Randall, Jr., on American and Soviet Philosophy." *Journal of Philosophy* 56 (23 Apr. 1959): 416-19.
    Reply to Randall, "The Mirror of USSR Philosophizing." Ibid. 55 (6 Nov. 1958): 1019-28.

"Philosophy and Human Conduct." *Philosophy East and West* 9 (Apr.-July 1959): 6-8.

"A Talk with Bhave." *New Leader* 42 (4 May 1959): 10-13.
[Reprinted in **Philosophy and Public Policy**, 1980.]

"A Talk with Vinoba Bhave." *Encounter* 12 (May 1959): 14-18.

"What's Left of Karl Marx?" *Saturday Review* 42 (6 June 1959): 12-14, 58.

"Pragmatism and Existentialism." *Antioch Review* 19 (Summer 1959): 151-68.

"'Common Sense' in Japan." *New Leader* 42 (5 Oct. 1959): 10-12.
[See "Which Way Japan?" 9 Feb. 1959.]

"John Dewey: His Philosophy of Education and Its Critics." *New Leader* 42 (2 Nov. 1959): Sec. 2.

"John Dewey: Philosopher of Growth." *Journal of Philosophy* 56 (17 Dec. 1959): 1010-18.
[Reprinted in **Education and the Taming of Power**, 1973.]

"The Ends and Content of Education." *Daedalus* 88 (Winter 1959): 7-24.
[Reprinted in **Education and the Taming of Power**, 1973.]

"Two Types of Existentialist Religion and Ethics." *Partisan Review* 26
(Winter 1959): 58-63.

1960

Dimensions of Mind, edited by Sidney Hook. Third Symposium, New York
University Institute of Philosophy, 15-16 May 1959. New York: New
York University Press, 1960.
[Reviewed in *Annals of the American Academy of Political and Social
Science* 332 (Nov. 1960): 163 (Edward Joseph Shoben, Jr.); *Christian
Century* 78 (26 July 1961): 904-5 (Albion Roy King); *Contemporary
Psychology* 6 (Apr. 1961): 124-25 (Albert H. Hastorf); *Cross Currents* 11
(Spring 1961): 159-63 (James Collins); *Ethics* 72 (Oct. 1961): 71 (V. C.
Chappell); *Library Journal* 85 (15 May 1960): 1920 (Harold Lancour);
Modern Schoolman 39 (Nov. 1961): 68-70 (Edward MacKinnon); *New
Leader* 44 (20 Feb. 1961): 25-26 (Frederick Schick); *Personalist* 42
(Spring 1961): 271-72 (J. P. Guilford); *Philosophy and Phenomenological
Research* 21 (June 1961): 577-78 (Jack Kaminsky); *Philosophy of Science*
29 (Apr. 1962): 218-20 (Irving Sosensky); *Review of Metaphysics* 14
(Sept. 1960): 177 (Daniel D. O'Connor); *Saturday Review* 43 (1 Oct.
1960): 25 (Thomas Hall); *Thought* 35 (Dec. 1960): 601-2 (J. Gerard
Bussy).]

"A Pragmatic Note." In **Dimensions of Mind**, edited by Sidney Hook, 202-
7. New York: New York University Press, 1960.

"To Free Gold and Sobell." Letter by Hook, Nathan Glazer, Irving Kristol,
and Dwight Macdonald. *New York Times*, 16 Feb. 1960, 36; *Progressive*
24 (Apr. 1960): 41-42.

"Of Tradition and Change." Review of **The Constitution of Liberty**, by
Friedrich August Hayek. *New York Times Book Review*, 21 Feb. 1960, 6,
28.

"Modern Knowledge and the Idea of God." *Commentary* 29 (Mar. 1960):
205-16.
[Reprinted in **The Quest for Being**, 1961.]

"A Handbook for the Years Ahead." Review of **The Future as History**, by
Robert L. Heilbroner. *Saturday Review* 43 (2 Apr. 1960): 22-23.

"Distrust of Soviet." *New York Times*, 5 Apr. 1960, 36.

Reply to David Riesman, "Toward Agreement on Tests." Ibid., 31 Mar. 1960, 32.
Response by Allan Brick, "Arming to Preserve Freedom." Ibid., 11 Apr. 1960, 30.

"A New Ism for Socialism." *New York Times Magazine*, 10 Apr. 1960, 13, 62, 64, 66, 69.

"Second Thoughts on Peace and Freedom." *New Leader* 43 (11 Apr. 1960): 8-12.
[See "A Foreign Policy for Survival," 7 Apr. 1958.]

"Soviet Writing." *Saturday Review* 43 (23 Apr. 1960): 27.
Reply to Alexander Chakovsky, "Russian Writing: A Soviet Editor's Report." Ibid. 43 (2 Apr. 1960): 12-14, 36-37.

"Carte-Blanche Legislative Authority." Review of **The People and the Court**, by Charles L. Black, Jr. *Saturday Review* 43 (30 Apr. 1960): 19-20.

"Bertrand Russell's Political Fantasies." *New Leader* 43 (9 May 1960): 15-17.
[See "A Foreign Policy for Survival," 7 Apr. 1958.]

"Was hat uns Karl Marx heute noch zu sagen?" *Politische Studien* 11 (June 1960): 364-70.

"Pragmatism and the Tragic Sense of Life." *Proceedings and Addresses of the American Philosophical Association* 33 (Oct. 1960): 5-26.
Condensed version in *Commentary* 30 (Aug. 1960): 139-49.
Reply by George Kimmelman, "Tragic, Aesthetic, Pragmatic." Ibid. 30 (Dec. 1960): 536.
Response by Hook, ibid.
[Reprinted in **Pragmatism and the Tragic Sense of Life**, 1974.]

"A Recollection of Berthold Brecht." *New Leader* 43 (10 Oct. 1960): 22-23.

"Scapegoat for Tyranny." Review of **Marxism: The View from America**, by Clinton Rossiter. *Saturday Review* 43 (12 Nov. 1960): 25-26.

"'Welfare State'--A Debate That Isn't." *New York Times Magazine*, 27 Nov. 1960, 27, 118-19.
Response by Marjorie H. Schefler, ibid., 11 Dec. 1960, 4.
Reply by Hook, ibid.
Replies by George Beiers and Donald B. Frazer, ibid.

"Philosophy and Human Conduct." *Kenyon Review* 22 (Fall 1960):
648-66.

"Visionary or Man of Vision?" *New Leader* 43 (12 Dec. 1960): 22-23.
Reply by Harry Gersh, "Hess and Judaism." Ibid. 44 (9 Jan. 1961):
30.

"Political Pretenders and How to Tell Them." *Saturday Review* 43 (31 Dec.
1960): 6-8, 29.

1961

The Quest for Being, and Other Studies in Naturalism and Humanism.
New York: St. Martin's Press, 1961.
[Reviewed in *Booklist* 51 (15 July 1961): 687; *Commentary* 33 (Feb.
1962): 143-51 (Henry David Aiken); *Ethics* 72 (Oct. 1961): 75; *Guardian*,
17 Nov. 1961, 8 (Stephen Toulmin); *Heythrop Journal* 3 (Apr. 1962): 197
(T. G.); *Humanist* 22 (Nov.-Dec. 1962): 201-3 (Gardner Williams);
Jewish Social Studies 30 (Jan. 1968): 60 (Leon J. Goldstein); *Journal of
Philosophy* 59 (21 June 1962): 355-59 (Frederick A. Olafson); *Kirkus* 29
(15 Mar. 1961): 288; *Library Journal* 86 (1 June 1961): 2109 (LaVern
Kohl); *Mind* 71 (Oct. 1962): 584-85 (Anthony Kenny); *New Leader* 45
(19 Feb. 1962): 26-27 (Gail Kennedy); *New Scholasticism* 36 (Oct. 1962):
557-60 (Andrew J. Reck); *New Statesman* 65 (4 Jan. 1963): 16 (George
Lichtheim); *New York Herald Tribune Books*, 10 Sept. 1961, 14; *New
York Times Book Review*, 18 June 1961, 7, 30 (Morton G. White);
Review of Metaphysics 15 (Sept. 1961): 192 (Richard J. Bernstein); *San
Francisco Chronicle, This World*, 22 Oct. 1961, 34 (J. W.); *Saturday
Review* 44 (22 July 1961): 26-27 (Richard J. Bernstein); *Time* 77 (9 June
1961): 89-90.]

Religious Experience and Truth, edited by Sidney Hook. Fourth
Symposium, New York University Institute of Philosophy, 21-22 Oct.
1960. New York: New York University Press, 1961.
[Reviewed in *Church Quarterly Review* 164 (Jan.-Mar. 1963): 106-7 (W.
R. Matthews); *Commonweal* 75 (2 Mar. 1962): 599-601 (Daniel Cal-
lahan); *Journal for the Scientific Study of Religion* 2 (Oct. 1962): 130-31
(Kirtley F. Mather); *Jubilee* 9 (Mar. 1962): 52; *Library Journal* 87 (15
Feb. 1962): 775 (LaVern Kohl); *Life of the Spirit* 17 (Jan. 1963): 293-94
(D. M. MacKinnon); *New York Times Book Review*, 28 Jan. 1962, 42
(Reinhold Niebuhr); *Philosophical Quarterly* 14 (Apr. 1964): 186-87
(Basil Mitchell); *Review of Metaphysics* 15 (June 1962): 683 (Eric
Walther); *Saturday Review* 45 (3 Feb. 1962): 23, 35 (Huston Smith);
Tablet 216 (31 Mar. 1962): 307 (Edward Quinn); *Theology Today* 20
(Jan. 1964): 583-85 (Paul L. Holmer).]

"The Atheism of Paul Tillich." In **Religious Experience and Truth,**
     edited by Sidney Hook, 59-64. New York: New York University Press,
     1961.
     [Reprinted in **Pragmatism and the Tragic Sense of Life,** 1974.]

"Diderot's Great Legacy." Review of **A Diderot Pictorial Encyclopedia of
     Trades and Industry.** *New Leader* 44 (2 Jan. 1961): 25-26.

"In Memoriam: S. M. Levitas." *New Leader* 44 (16 Jan. 1961): 3-4.

"The Ethics of Controversy: Rejoinder to Julius Stone." *Observer,* 18 Mar.
     1961.

"The Death Sentence." *New Leader* 44 (3 Apr. 1961): 18-20.
     Reply by Hugo Adam Bedau, ibid. 44 (8 May 1961): 28.

"Each Man for Himself." Review of **For the New Intellectual: The
     Philosophy of Ayn Rand,** by Ayn Rand. *New York Times Book Review,* 9
     Apr. 1961, 3. Correction, ibid., 23 Apr. 1961, 44.
          Letters in response by Andrew E. Carlan, Allan Blumenthal, and
               John V. Rohr, Jr., ibid., 7 May 1961, 34-35.
          Reply by Hook, ibid., 35.

"The Couch and the Bomb." *New Leader* 44 (24 Apr. 1961): 6-9.
          Replies by Zbigniew K. Brzezinski, Bernard Herman, and Paul
               Lauter, ibid. 44 (8 May 1961): 27-28.
          Reply by Erich Fromm, ibid. 44 (29 May 1961): 10-12.
          Response by Hook, "Escape from Reality." Ibid., 12-14.
          Correction to Hook's "Escape from Reality." Ibid. 44 (5 June
               1961): 22.
          Response by Maximilien Rubel, ibid. 44 (12 June 1961): 30.
          Reply by Hook, ibid., 30.
          Response by B. K. Harper to Fromm, ibid. 44 (19 June 1961): 29.
          Response by Rubel, ibid. 44 (31 July-7 Aug. 1961): 29.
          Response by Hook, ibid.

"Growth of Pacifism Noted." *New York Times,* 2 May 1961, 36.

"In League with the Kremlin." Review of **American Commissar,** by Sandor
     Voros. *Saturday Review* 44 (20 May 1961): 38-39.

"Split Decisions." Review of **Justices Black and Frankfurter: Conflict in
     the Court,** by Wallace Mendelson. *New York Times Book Review,* 23
     July 1961, 6, 26.

"Questions of Conformity." Letter to the editor. *New Republic* 145 (21

Aug. 1961): 30-31.
> Reply to Irving Howe, ibid. 145 (3 July 1961): 25-26.
> Reply by Howe, ibid. 145 (21 Aug. 1961): 31.

"For Stand at West Berlin. Author Assails View That Policy of Containment Be Abolished." Letter to the editor. *New York Times*, 28 Aug. 1961, 24.
> Reply to Erich Kahler, ibid., 18 Aug. 1961, 20.
> Reply by Norman Thomas, "To Defend West Berlin." Ibid., 1 Sept. 1961, 16.

"Enlightenment and Radicalism." *Encounter* 17 (Aug. 1961): 44-50.
Also printed in **History and Hope**, 59-67, with comments by Hook, ibid., 135-36, 156-58. Congress for Cultural Freedom, Berlin, 1960. London: Routledge and Kegan Paul, 1962.
[Reprinted in **Pragmatism and the Tragic Sense of Life**, 1974.]

"The New Revisionism." Review of **The History of the Cold War**, by John Lukacs. *East Europe* 10 (Aug. 1961): 19, 48-49.
> Reply by Lukacs, ibid. 10 (Oct. 1961): 39, 51.
> Response by Hook, ibid., 51.

Contributions to "Symposium on Capital Punishment." *New York Law Forum* 7 (Aug. 1961): 249-319. [Hook's contribution, 278-83, 296-99, 300.]

"'Unless We Resist.'" *Time*, 8 Sept. 1961, 22.

"Western Values and Total War." A panel discussion by Hook, H. Stuart Hughes, Hans J. Morganthau, and C. P. Snow. *Commentary* 32 (Oct. 1961): 277-304.
> Comment on discussion by William F. Rickenbacker, "Schism of the Left." *National Review* 11 (15 July 1961): 8.

"After Berlin--What Next." *Nation's Business* 49 (Oct. 1961): 59-60.

"Marx and Alienation." *New Leader* 44 (11 Dec. 1961): 15-18.

1962

The Paradoxes of Freedom. Berkeley: University of California Press, 1962.
[Reviewed in *Annals of the American Academy of Political and Social Science* 350 (Nov. 1963): 211-12 (John D. Lewis); *California Law Review* 51 (Mar. 1963): 255-60 (Martin Shapiro); *Commentary* 35 (Mar. 1963): 260-62 (Lewis A. Coser); *Forum Service* no. 585 (16 Mar. 1963): 1-4

(Daniel Bell); *Humanist* 24 (Jan.-Feb. 1964): 19-20 (Van Meter Ames); ibid., 20 (William Van Alstyne); *Jewish Social Studies* 27 (Oct. 1965): 262-63 (Joseph L. Blau); *Journal of Church and State* 6 (Winter 1964): 90-94 (William G. Toland); *Journal of Philosophy* 62 (29 Apr. 1965): 241-46 (Arnold S. Kaufman); *Library Journal* 87 (15 Sept. 1962): 3053 (Thomas M. Bogie); *New Leader* 46 (18 Feb. 1963): 24-25 (Wallace Mendelson); *New Statesman* 65 (4 Jan. 1963): 16 (George Lichtheim); *New York Times Book Review*, 7 Oct. 1962, 6, 34 (John Cogley); *New York University Law Review* 38 (Jan. 1963): 200-203 (Henry H. Foster, Jr.); *Progressive* 27 (Mar. 1963): 43-44 (David Fellman); *Saturday Review* 46 (13 Apr. 1963): 80 (Charles A. Madison); *UCLA Law Review* 10 (1962-63): 965-84 (Bruno Leoni); *University of Chicago Law Review* 30 (Autumn 1962): 191-97 (Philip B. Kurland).]

From Hegel to Marx. With a new introduction by Hook. Ann Arbor: University of Michigan Press, 1962.
[Reviewed in *New Statesman* 65 (4 Jan. 1963): 16 (George Lichtheim); *Slavic and East European Journal* 7 (Winter 1963): 437-38 (Donald S. Carlisle).]

World Communism, edited by Sidney Hook. Princeton, N.J.: Van Nostrand, 1962.

"Hegel and the Perspective of Liberalism." In **A Hegel Symposium**, edited by Don C. Travis, 39-62. Austin: University of Texas, 1962.
[Reprinted in **Pragmatism and the Tragic Sense of Life**, 1974.]

"The Humanities and the Taming of Power." In **The Role of the Humanities in Ordering a Peaceful World**, 5-21. New Britain: Central Connecticut State College, 1962.

Introduction to **The Soviet Revolution, 1917-1939**, by Raphael R. Abramovitch, vii-xii. New York: International Universities Press, 1962.

"Philosophy and Human Conduct." In **Philosophy and Culture--East and West**, edited by Charles A. Moore, 15-32. Honolulu: University of Hawaii Press, 1962.

"Better Red Than Dead, or Lord Russell's Guide to Peace." Review of **Has Man a Future?** by Bertrand Russell. *New York Times Book Review*, 14 Jan. 1962, 44.
Replies by Julian Koslow, Paul Goodman, J. Ernest Bryant, and M. Lincoln Schuster, ibid., 18 Feb. 1962, 42-43.
Response by Hook, ibid., 43.

"Revisionism at Bay." *Encounter* 19 (Sept. 1962): 63-67.

Review of **Philosophy and Myth in Karl Marx**, by Robert C. Tucker. *Slavic Review* 21 (Sept. 1962): 552-53.

"Communism: What Lies Ahead." *Nation's Business* 50 (Oct. 1962): 62, 64, 66, 68.

"The Map Was Redrawn to Make Man's Agony a Part of the Geography." Review of **Being and Time**, by Martin Heidegger, translated by John Macquarrie and Edward Robinson. *New York Times Book Review*, 11 Nov. 1962, 6, 42.

"The Politics of Science Fiction." Review of **Fail-Safe**, by Eugene Burdick and Harvey Wheeler. *New Leader* 45 (10 Dec. 1962): 12-15.

"The Impact of Expanding Research Support on the Universities." *Journal of Medical Education* 37 (Dec. 1962): 230-46.

"The Cold War and the West." A symposium with Hook et al. *Partisan Review* 29 (Winter 1962): 20-27.

1963

Education for Modern Man: A New Perspective. New York: Alfred A. Knopf, 1963.

The Fail-Safe Fallacy. New York: Stein and Day, 1963.
[Reviewed in *Book Week* 1 (27 Oct. 1963): 4 (Gerald Wendt); *Library Journal* 88 (15 Oct. 1963): 3856 (Bernard Poll); *National Review* 15 (19 Nov. 1963): 444-45 (Jameson G. Campaigne, Jr.); *New York Times*, 14 Oct. 1963, 27 (Harrison E. Salisbury); *New York Times Book Review*, 6 Oct. 1963, 3 (Mark S. Watson); *Virginia Quarterly Review* 40 (Winter 1964): xlii.]

Philosophy and History, edited by Sidney Hook. Fifth Symposium, New York University Institute of Philosophy, 11-12 May 1962. New York: New York University Press, 1963.
[Reviewed in *American Historical Review* 69 (Oct. 1963): 83-84 (William Gerber); *Bibliographie de la Philosophie* 11 (1964): 199-200 (Paul Kurtz); *Christian Century* 80 (20 Nov. 1963): 1436 (William A. Sadler, Jr.); *Ethics* 74 (July 1964): 302-4 (Frank H. Knight); *History and Theory* 4 (1965): 328-49 (Marvin Levich); *International Philosophical Quarterly* 4 (Feb. 1964): 320-22 (Eugene Fontinell); *Journal of the History of Ideas* 25 (Oct.-Dec. 1964): 587-98 (Frank H. Knight); *Mind* 74 (July 1965): 434-38 (W. H. Walsh); *Mississippi Valley Historical Review* 50 (June 1963): 155; *Personalist* 44 (Autumn 1963): 549-50 (William H. Werkmeister); *Re-*

view of Metaphysics 18 (Dec. 1964): 389 (Charles E. Butterworth); *Wisconsin Magazine of History* 48 (Summer 1965): 327-28 (William Fletcher Thompson, Jr.).]

"Objectivity and Reconstruction in History." In **Philosophy and History**, edited by Sidney Hook, 250-75. New York: New York University Press, 1963.

"Summary of the Symposium." In **The Health Care Issues of the 1960's**, 179-99. New York: Group Health Insurance, 1963.

Introduction to **The True Believer**, by Eric Hoffer, xix-xxv. New York: Time, 1963.

"'Lord Monboddo' and the Supreme Court." Review of **One Man's Stand for Freedom**, edited by Irving Dilliard. *New Leader* 46 (13 May 1963): 11-15.
> Reply by Leon H. Keyserling, "Justice Black." Ibid. 46 (10 June 1963): 31-32.
> Response by Hook, ibid., 32-33.
> Reply by Keyserling, "Justice Black (Cont.)." Ibid. 46 (24 June 1963): 33.
> Response by Hook, ibid., 33-34.

"Do the People Rule and Can They?" Review of **The Essential Lippmann: A Political Philosophy for Liberal Democracy**, by Walter Lippmann, edited by Clinton Rossiter and James Lare. *New York Times Book Review*, 14 July 1963, 1, 24, 25.
> Responses by Landon Gerald Dowdey, Robert D. Masters, Jerome Zukosky, Ralph S. Berendt, Thomas H. B. Robertson, and Victor R. Thayer, ibid., 8 Sept. 1963, 32.
> Reply by Hook, ibid.

"Test-Ban Treaty." *New Leader* 46 (16 Sept. 1963): 24-25.
> Reply to Norman Jacobs, "Freezing the Balance of Terror." Ibid. 46 (5 Aug. 1963): 8-9.
> Response by Jacobs, ibid. 46 (16 Sept. 1963): 26.

"Why the U.S. Needs a Freedom Academy." *Think* 29 (Sept. 1963): 6-9.

"Challenging Study: Challenge of Communism." *New York Times Magazine*, 13 Oct. 1963, 25, 33, 34, 38, 41.
> Reply by Louis Fischer, ibid., 27 Oct. 1963, 12.
> Response by Hook, ibid.

"Religious Liberty from the Viewpoint of the Open Society." *Cross Currents*

13 (Winter 1963): 65-75.

"American Philosophy Today." *America* 68 (1963): 27-34.

1964

Law and Philosophy, edited by Sidney Hook. Sixth Symposium, New York
University Institute of Philosophy, 10-11 May 1963. New York: New
York University Press, 1964.
[Reviewed in *Catholic Lawyer* 11 (Summer 1965): 263-64 (Patrick J.
Rohan); *Choice* 2 (May 1965): 192; *Christian Century* 81 (4 Nov. 1964):
1372; *International Philosophical Quarterly* 5 (May 1965): 311-16
(Thomas F. McGann); *Nation* 200 (12 Apr. 1965): 398-401 (Hugo Adam
Bedau); *New York Times Book Review*, 22 Nov. 1964, 10 (Fred Rodell;
letters and Rodell's reply, ibid., 20 Dec. 1964, 12-13); *Review of
Metaphysics* 19 (Dec. 1965): 389 (Edward A. Reno, Jr.).]

"Preface" and "Law, Justice, and Obedience." In **Law and Philosophy**,
edited by Sidney Hook, xi-xiii, 56-60. New York: New York University
Press, 1964.

"Conversations of Professors Hook, Dallin and Bell." In **World Politics**,
edited by Māhir Nasīm. Cairo: Dar Al-kurrnek, 1964.

"The Death Sentence." In **The Death Penalty in America**, edited by Hugo
Adam Bedau, 146-54. Chicago: Aldine, 1964.

Introduction to **A Preface to Morals**, by Walter Lippmann, new ed., xv-xxii.
New York: Time-Life Books, 1964.

"Intelligence and Human Rights." In **Memorias del XIII Congreso Inter-
nacional de Filosofía**, VII, 101-2. México: Universidad Nacional
Autónoma de México, 1964.

"Religious Liberty from the Viewpoint of a Secular Humanist." In **Religious Conflict in America**, by Earl Raab, 138-51. Garden City, N.Y.:
Doubleday and Co., 1964.

"Liberalism and the Negro: A Round-Table Discussion." With James Bald-
win, Nathan Glazer, and Gunnar Myrdal. *Commentary* 37 (Mar. 1964):
25-42.

"Fail-Safe, &c." Letter to the editor. *New York Review of Books* 2 (2 Apr.
1964): 17.
Reply to Robert Brustein's review of the movie *Dr. Strangelove*.

Ibid. 1 (6 Feb. 1964): 3-4.
Comment by Kenneth Stern, "Strangelove & Fail-Safe." Ibid. 2 (5
Mar. 1964): 18.
Reply by Brustein, ibid.

"Fulbright's Rights Stand." *New York Times*, 8 Apr. 1964, 42.
Reply by J. A. Fabro, ibid., 13 Apr. 1964, 28.

"Pornography and the Censor." *New York Times Book Review*, 12 Apr.
1964, 1, 38-39.
Responses by Elmer Rice, Robert W. Haney et al., ibid., 10 May
1964, 32-33.
Reply by Hook, ibid., 33.

"The Cunning of History." Review of **The Prophet Outcast**, by Isaac
Deutscher. *New Leader* 47 (11 May 1964): 15-18.
Correction, ibid. 47 (25 May 1964): 35.
Response by Max Nomad, ibid. 47 (22 June 1964): 32-33.
Reply by Hook, ibid., 33.
[Reprinted in **Philosophy and Public Policy**, 1980.]

"Common Sense and Disarmament." *Yale Political* 3 (Spring 1964): 16, 29-
30.

"Hegel e le prospettive del liberalismo." *De Homine*, nos. 9-10 (June 1964):
115-40.

"There's More Than One Way To Teach." *Saturday Review* 47 (18 July
1964): 48-49, 59.

"Thinking about Thinkers of the Unthinkable." Review of **Strategy and
Conscience**, by Anatol Rapoport. *New York Times Book Review*, 19 July
1964, 6, 25.
Responses by Hilbert Schenck, Jr., A. Mowshowitz, Michael I. Sobel,
and B. L. Winter, ibid., 6 Sept. 1964, 18.
Reply by Hook, ibid.

"A Search Here and Beyond." Review of **Cold Friday**, by Whittaker Chambers, edited by Duncan Norton-Taylor. *New York Times Book Review*, 8
Nov. 1964, 3, 32.

"Faces of Betrayers." Review of **The New Meaning of Treason**, by Rebecca
West. *New York Times Book Review*, 29 Nov. 1964, 1, 60-61.

Review of **Charles Peirce and Scholastic Realism: A Study of Peirce's
Relation to John Duns Scotus**, by John F. Boler. *Bibliography of*

Philosophy 11 (1964): 100.

Review of **True Love, True Humour and True Religion: A Semantic Study**, by Sören Halldén. *Bibliography of Philosophy* 11 (1964): 208.

Review of **Metaphysics and Historicity**, by Emil L. Fackenheim. *History and Theory* 3 (1964): 389-92.

1965

Reason, Social Myths, and Democracy. With a new introduction by Hook. New York: Harper and Row, 1965.

Introduction to **The New Meaning of Treason**, by Rebecca West, new ed., xv-xx. New York: Time-Life Books, 1965.

"Academic Freedom and the Rights of Students." In **The Berkeley Student Revolt**, edited by Seymour Martin Lipset and Sheldon S. Wolin, 432-42. Garden City, N.Y.: Anchor Books, 1965.

"The Political Aspects of General and Complete Disarmament." In **The Prospects for Arms Control**, edited by James E. Dougherty and John F. Lehman, Jr., 153-63. New York: Macfadden-Bartell, 1965.

"Second Thoughts on Berkeley." In **Revolution at Berkeley**, edited by Michael V. Miller and Susan Gilmore, 116-59. New York: Dial Press, 1965.
[Reprinted in **Academic Freedom and Academic Anarchy**, 1970.]

"Freedom to Learn but Not to Riot." *New York Times Magazine*, 3 Jan. 1965, 1, 8, 9, 16, 18.
     Replies by Paul Goodman, Lawrence D. Hochman, Harold Leitenberg, and Kay Boyle, ibid., 17 Jan. 1965, 6, 21.
     Response by Hook, ibid., 21.

"Hegel Rehabilitated?" *Encounter* 24 (Jan. 1965): 53-58.
     Reply by Shlomo Avineri, "Hook's Hegel." Ibid. 25 (Nov. 1965): 63-66.
     Reply by Z. A. Pelczynski, "Hegel Again." Ibid. 26 (Mar. 1966): 47-50.
     Rejoinder by Hook, "Hegel & His Apologists." Ibid. 26 (May 1966): 84-91.

"Defends Protests to Russia on Jews." *New York Times*, 13 Feb. 1965, 20.
     Response to Stephen P. Dunn, "Anti-Semitism in Soviet." Ibid., 25 Jan. 1965, 36.

"Changing Values in Higher Education in a Changing Society." *New York State Education* 52 (Feb. 1965): 6-9.

"Reply to Dr. Oppenheimer." *Denver Post*, 27 July 1965, 19.
> Reply to Frank Oppenheimer's letter on U.S. policy toward communism, ibid., 6 June 1965, 51.

"Friends and Enemies." Review of **Oppenheimer: The Story of a Friendship**, by Haakon Chevalier. *New York Times Book Review*, 22 Aug. 1965, 3, 28.
> Reply by Chevalier, ibid., 19 Sept. 1965, 52.
> Response by Hook, ibid., 52-53.

"The Philosophy of American Pragmatism." *Span* 6 (Aug. 1965): 21-28.

"Truth and Consequences." *Partisan Review* 32 (Summer 1965): 485-86.
> Reply to G. S. Fraser, "Impolite Essays." Ibid. 32 (Winter 1965): 127-33.
> Reply by Fraser, ibid. 32 (Summer 1965): 486-87.

"Radicalism in America." *New Leader* 48 (27 Sept. 1965): 34-35.
> Reply to John P. Roche, "Profiles in 'Tsoores.'" Ibid. 48 (16 Aug. 1965): 14-16.
> Reply to Christopher Lasch, "Radicalism in America." Ibid. 48 (13 Sept. 1965): 33.

"The Conflict of Freedoms." *Common Factor* 1 (Autumn 1965): 36-42.

1966

Art and Philosophy, edited by Sidney Hook. Seventh Symposium, New York University Institute of Philosophy, 23-24 Oct. 1964. New York: New York University Press, 1966.
[Reviewed in *British Journal of Aesthetics* 6 (July 1966): 303; *Dalhousie Review* 46 (Autumn 1966): 390-91 (Geoffrey Payzant); *Foundations of Language* 5 (Nov. 1969): 567-68 (J. J. A. Mooij); *Journal of Aesthetics and Art Criticism* 25 (Summer 1967): 478 (David Thoreau Wieck); *Journal of the History of Philosophy* 6 (Oct. 1968): 416-17 (John M. Walker); *Music and Letters* 47 (July 1966): 269 (F. H.); *New Statesman* 72 (9 Sept. 1966): 367-68 (Richard Wollheim); *Philosophy and Phenomenological Research* 28 (Sept. 1967): 137-38 (Jerome Stolnitz); *Review of Metaphysics* 20 (Sept. 1966): 163 (R. J. Woods); *Saturday Review* 49 (11 June 1966): 60, 62 (George W. Linden); *Southern Review* 4 (July 1968): 766 (Robert Hollander).]

"Preface" and "Are There Universal Criteria of Judgments of Excellence in Art?" In **Art and Philosophy**, edited by Sidney Hook, ix-x, 49-55. New York: New York University Press, 1966.

"A Philosopher's View." In **Man's Quest for Security**, edited by E. J. Faulkner, 1-17. Lincoln: University of Nebraska Press, 1966.
Comment by Charles H. Patterson, ibid., 18-24.

"Marxism in the Western World: From 'Scientific Socialism' to Mythology." In **Marxist Ideology in the Contemporary World--Its Appeals and Paradoxes**, edited by Milorad M. Drachkovitch, 1-36. Published for the Hoover Institution on War, Revolution, and Peace. New York: Frederick A. Praeger, 1966.
[Reprinted in **Revolution, Reform, and Social Justice**, 1975.]

"Thoughts after Knopfelmacher." *Minerva* 4 (Winter 1966): 279-85.
Reply to A. K. Stout, "On University Appointments: Thoughts after Knopfelmacher." Ibid. 4 (Autumn 1965): 55-72.

"In Reply to Dr. Hutchins." Letter to the editor. *Santa Barbara News-Press*, 27 Feb. 1966, C-8, C-9.

"Hook Answers Hutchins." *Los Angeles Times*, 12 Mar. 1966, pt. 3, 4.
Reply to Robert M. Hutchins, "The President Should Offer Some Specifics." Ibid., 7 Mar. 1966, pt. 2, 5.
Reply by Harold Willens, ibid., 26 Mar. 1966, pt. 3, 4.
Response by Hook, "Writer Buttresses His Previous Criticism of Tax-Exempt Center." Ibid., 4 Apr. 1966, pt. 2, 4.

"U.S. Policy and Communism." *Santa Barbara News-Press*, 20 Mar. 1966, C-9.

"Liberal Catholic Thought." Review of **Belief and Unbelief**, by Michael Novak. *Commentary* 41 (Apr. 1966): 94-100.

Letter. *New York Times Magazine*, 8 May 1966, 22.
Reply to Lewis S. Feuer, "American Philosophy Is Dead." Ibid., 24 Apr. 1966, 30-31, 122, 124.

"Karl Marx's Second Coming." *New York Times Book Review*, 22 May 1966, 2, 44-45.
Response by L. Marcus, ibid., 10 July 1966, 50.
Reply by Hook, ibid., 50-51.

"Neither Blind Obedience nor Uncivil Disobedience." *New York Times*

Magazine, 5 June 1966, 52-53, 122-28.
>Reply by R. W. Tucker, "A Bitter Lesson." Ibid., 19 June 1966, 4.
>Reply by Samuel H. Hofstadter, ibid., 4, 49.

"Lord Russell and the War Crimes 'Trial.'" *New Leader* 49 (24 Oct. 1966): 6-11.
>Reply by Ralph Schoenman, "Lord Russell's 'Tribunal.'" Ibid. 49 (19 Dec. 1966): 27-28.
>Response by Hook, ibid., 28.
>[Reprinted in **Philosophy and Public Policy**, 1980.]

"Some Educational Attitudes and Poses." *Harvard Educational Review* 36 (Fall 1966): 496-504.
>[Reprinted in **Education and the Taming of Power**, 1973.]

"Liberties in Conflict." Review of **Toward a General Theory of the First Amendment**, by Thomas I. Emerson. *Chicago Sun-Times Book Week*, 6 Nov. 1966, 5, 10.

1967

Religion in a Free Society. Lincoln: University of Nebraska Press, 1967; Don Mills, Ontario: Burns and MacEachern, 1967.
>[Reviewed in *Ave Maria* 105 (13 May 1967): 11 (Donald McDonald); *Booklist* 63 (15 July 1967): 1168-69; *Catholic Library World* 39 (Nov. 1967): 246; *Choice* 5 (Mar. 1968): 70; *Christian Century* 84 (30 Aug. 1967): 1104, 1106 (John M. Swomley, Jr.); *Harvard Educational Review* 38 (Spring 1968): 396-403 (William Buss); *Journal of Church and State* 12 (Autumn 1970): 497-500 (William G. Toland); *Journal of Value Inquiry* 2 (Winter 1968): 308-14 (Marvin Fox); *Religion and the Public Order* no. 5 (1969): 183-84 (Thomas J. O'Toole); *Religious Humanism* 2 (Winter 1968): 91 (James H. Hutchinson); *Review of Religious Research* 11 (Fall 1969): 92-93 (Eugene A. Mainelli); *Saturday Review* 50 (21 Oct. 1967): 82 (John Calam); *Stanford Law Review* 20 (Nov. 1967): 146-47 (Walter F. Berns).]

Human Values and Economic Policy, edited by Sidney Hook. Eighth Symposium, New York University Institute of Philosophy, 13-14 May 1966. New York: New York University Press, 1967.
>[Reviewed in *American Economic Review* 58 (Dec. 1968): 1384-85 (Kurt Klappholz); *Choice* 6 (June 1969): 550; *Critique* 35 (Apr. 1969): 359-76 (Bernard Cazes); *Economic Journal* (London) 80 (Mar. 1970): 122-23 (C. W. Guillebaud); *Library Journal* 92 (1 Oct. 1967): 3413 (Richard A. Gray).]

"Preface" and "Basic Values and Economic Policy." In **Human Values and Economic Policy**, edited by Sidney Hook, ix-x, 246-55. New York: New York University Press, 1967.

"On the Couch." Review of **Friendship and Fratricide**, by Meyer A. Zeligs. *New York Times Book Review*, 5 Feb. 1967, 4, 40, 41.
     Response by Zeligs, ibid., 19 Mar. 1967, 59-60.
     Reply by Hook, ibid., 60-61.
     Response by Marshall A. Best, ibid., 2 Apr. 1967, 44.

"Le deuxième avènement de Marx." *Le Contrat Social* 11 (Mar.-Apr. 1967): 91-94.

"Whither Russia? Fifty Years After." *Problems of Communism* 16 (Mar.-Apr. 1967): 76-79.

"What's Happening to America (Round II)." *Partisan Review* 34 (Spring 1967): 254-63.

"Lessons of the Hungarian 'October.'" *Scope* 3 (Spring-Autumn 1967): 1-3.

"Topical Comment: Race Violence. Crisis for White, Negro Leadership." *Los Angeles Times*, 28 July 1967, pt. 2, 5.

"Cruel Deception." Letter to the editor. *New Leader* 50 (14 Aug. 1967): 26-27.
     Reply by M. S. Arnoni on the Vietnamese conflict, ibid. 50 (25 Sept. 1967): 26-27.
     Response by Hook, ibid., 27.
     Reply by Arnoni, ibid. 50 (23 Oct. 1967): 34.
     Rejoinder by Hook, ibid., 34-35.

"Topical Comment: Black Power, U.S.A. Is There a Legal 'Right' to Revolt?" *Los Angeles Times*, 15 Aug. 1967, pt. 2, 5.

"Fluff on the Sleeve of History." Review of **Variety of Men**, by C. P. Snow. *New Leader* 50 (28 Aug. 1967): 16-18.

"Fulbright's Colossal Gall." *Providence Journal*, 4 Sept. 1967, 57.

"Liberal Anti-Communism Revisited: A Symposium." With Lionel Abel et al. *Commentary* 44 (Sept. 1967): 44-48.

'Social Protest and Civil Obedience." *Humanist* 27 (Sept.-Dec. 1967): 157-

59, 192-93.
[Reprinted in **Revolution, Reform, and Social Justice**, 1975.]

"The Fiedler Fund." Letter by Hook et al. *Partisan Review* 34 (Fall 1967): 650.

"The Human Cost [of Soviet Industrialization following the 1917 Revolution]." *New Leader* 50 (6 Nov. 1967): 16-20.

"Does Philosophy Have a Future?" *Saturday Review* 50 (11 Nov. 1967): 21-23, 62.

"A Right Way to Remedy a Wrong, a Wrong Way to Remedy a Right." *New York Times Magazine*, 26 Nov. 1967, 124, 126.

1968

Contemporary Philosophy. Chicago: American Library Association, 1968.

"In Defense of 'Justice.'" In **Ethics and Social Justice**, edited by Howard E. Kiefer and Milton K. Munitz, 75-84. Vol. 4 of Contemporary Philosophic Thought: The International Philosophy Year Conferences at Brockport. Albany: State University of New York Press, 1968.
    Response to Walter Kaufmann, "Doubts About Justice." Ibid., 52-74.
[Reprinted in **Philosophy and Public Policy**, 1980.]

"Reflections on Human Rights." In **Ethics and Social Justice**, edited by Howard E. Kiefer and Milton K. Munitz, 252-81. Vol. 4 of Contemporary Philosophic Thought: The International Philosophy Year Conferences at Brockport. Albany: State University of New York Press, 1968.
[Reprinted in **Philosophy and Public Policy**, 1980.]

"The Democratic Challenge to Communism." In **Fifty Years of Communism in Russia**, edited by Milorad M. Drachkovitch, 284-92. Hoover Institution Publication no. 77. University Park: Pennsylvania State University Press, 1968.

"Human Rights and Social Justice." In **Social Justice and the Problems of the Twentieth Century**, by Sidney Hook, Tom Wicker, and C. Vann Woodward, 7-23. Raleigh: North Carolina State University, 1968.
[Reprinted in **Revolution, Reform, and Social Justice**, 1975.]

"Introduction. A Chapter in American Radical History: V. F. Calverton and His Periodicals." In reprint of *Modern Quarterly*, vol. 1, 1923-1924 (New York: Greenwood Reprint Corporation, 1968), 6pp.

"The University Law School." In **The Law School of Tomorrow**, edited by David Haber and Julius Cohen, 38-55. New Brunswick, N.J.: Rutgers University Press, 1968.
> Comment on speech by Robert M. Hutchins, ibid., 5-24.

"The Ethics of Political Controversy" and "Discussion." In **The Ethics of Controversy: Politics and Protest**. Proceedings of the First Annual Symposium on Issues in Public Communication, University of Kansas, 27-28 June 1968, 50-71, 72-85.

"The Human Costs of Revolution." *Survey* 66 (Jan. 1968): 129-37.
> [Reprinted in **Revolution, Reform, and Social Justice**, 1975.]

"The Enlightenment and Marxism." *Journal of the History of Ideas* 29 (Jan.-Mar. 1968): 93-108.
> [Reprinted in **Revolution, Reform, and Social Justice**, 1975.]

"Public Strikes." Letter to the editor. *New York Times*, 9 Feb. 1968, 26.

"Student Revolts Could Destroy Academic Freedom." *New York University Alumni News*, May 1968, 8-9.
> [Reprinted in **In Defense of Academic Freedom**, 1971.]

"America Must Erase the Cult of Violence." *Newsday*, 6 June 1968, 44.

"Civil Liberties Issue in Appointment." *New York Times*, 1 Aug. 1968, 30.
> Reply by Donald D. Shack, "Academic Freedom Called Issue." Ibid., 6 Aug. 1968, 36.

"Political Thinking Beyond Politics." Review of **Toward a Marxist Humanism**, by Leszek Kolakowski. *New York Times Book Review*, 1 Sept. 1968, 8, 25.

"N.Y.U. vs. Hatchett." *New York Times*, 28 Oct. 1968, 46.

"Academic Freedom and Academic Anarchy." *Survey* 69 (Oct. 1968): 62-75.

"Marcusian Values." *New York Times Magazine*, 10 Nov. 1968, 22.
> Reply to Herbert Marcuse interview, "Marcuse Defines His New Left Line." Ibid., 27 Oct. 1968, 29-31, 87, 89, 90, 92, 97, 99, 100, 109.
> Letters by Lester G. Crocker, Algirdas Landbergis, and Richard C. Michel, ibid., 17 Nov. 1968, 12.

"Sidney Hook Replies." Letter to the editor. *New York Post*, 19 Nov. 1968, 56.
> Reply to Murray Kempton, "Sidney Hook and Company." Ibid., 14 Nov. 1968, 53.

Letter to the editor. *Atlantic Monthly* 222 (Dec. 1968): 42-44.
> Reply to Martin Duberman, "On Misunderstanding Student Rebels."
> Ibid. 222 (Nov. 1968): 63-70.
> Comments by William Capitman et al., ibid. 223 (Jan. 1969): 28-31.

1969

Language and Philosophy, edited by Sidney Hook. Ninth Symposium, New
York University Institute of Philosophy, 1968. New York: New York
University Press, 1969.
[Reviewed in *Canadian Journal of Linguistics* 14 (Spring 1969): 142-43
(Zeno Vendler); *Dialogue* 8 (Dec. 1969): 523-26 (Douglas Odegard);
Encounter 36 (1971): 87 (Peter Hacker); *Forum for Modern Language
Studies* 7 (Oct. 1971): 413; *Journal of Linguistics* 6 (Feb. 1970): 134-36
(L. Jonathan Cohen); *Journal of Value Inquiry* 4 (Fall 1970): 235-37 (G.
Benjamin Oliver); *Linguistics* 111 (1 Sept. 1973): 99-115 (Venera
Mihailescu-Urechia); *Philosophischen Literaturanzeigers* 25 (1972): 115-
17 (Agehananda Bharati); *Queen's Quarterly* 77 (Winter 1970): 653-54
(P. W. Rogers); *Times* (London) *Literary Supplement* 3,616 (18 June
1971): 717.]

The Essential Thomas Paine, edited by Sidney Hook. New York: New
American Library, [1969].

"Introduction" and "Empiricism, Rationalism, and Innate Ideas." In **Language and Philosophy**, edited by Sidney Hook, ix-xi, 160-67. New York:
New York University Press, 1969.

"Absolutism and Human Rights." In **Philosophy, Science, and Method:
Essays in Honor of Ernest Nagel**, edited by Sidney Morgenbesser,
Patrick Suppes, and Morton G. White, 382-99. New York: St. Martin's
Press, 1969.
[Reprinted in **Pragmatism and the Tragic Sense of Life**, 1974.]

"The Trojan Horse in American Higher Education." *Educational Record* 50
(Winter 1969): 21-29.
> Reply by Hook to comments by Jerome Shaffer et al., "Prof. Hook
> Replies to His Critics." *Connecticut Daily Campus*, 4 Feb. 1969.
> Response by Hook to further comments by Shaffer et al., "Professor
> Hook Replies." Ibid., 24 Feb. 1969, 2.
[Reprinted in **Academic Freedom and Academic Anarchy**, 1970.]

"Brecht." *New Leader* 52 (3 Feb. 1969): 34.
> Reply to Eric Russell Bentley's comment on Richard Pipes's review
> of **The Great Terror**, by Robert Conquest. Ibid. 51 (2 Dec.

1968): 6-8; ibid. 51 (30 Dec. 1968): 29.
Reply by Conquest, ibid. 52 (3 Mar. 1969): 35.
Rebuttal by Bentley, ibid. 52 (17 Mar. 1969): 34-35.
Response by Hook, ibid. 52 (28 Apr. 1969): 34-35.
Response by Henry M. Pachter, ibid., 35.

"The War against the Democratic Process." *Atlantic* 223 (Feb. 1969): 45-49.
Responses by Hubert T. Davis, Charles Newlin, Helen L. Smith, William M. Lunch, J. Salamon, Mary Risk Hine, ibid. 223 (Apr. 1969): 44-46.
Reply by Hook, ibid., 46-47.

"Some Reflections on the Encyclopedia of Philosophy." *Religious Humanism* 3 (Winter 1969): 4-7.

"Reason and Violence--Some Truths and Myths about John Dewey." *Humanist* 29 (Mar.-Apr. 1969): center sec., 4 pp.
[Reprinted in **Education and the Taming of Power**, 1973.]

"Who Is Responsible for Campus Violence?" *Saturday Review* 52 (19 Apr. 1969): 22-25, 54-55.
[Reprinted in **Academic Freedom and Academic Anarchy**, 1970.]

"Help Wanted--Superman." Review of **An Essay on Liberation**, by Herbert Marcuse. *New York Times Book Review*, 20 Apr. 1969, 8.

"What Are the University Centers for Rational Alternatives?" *Measure* no. 1 (Apr. 1969): 2.

"The Real Crisis on the Campus: A Noted Educator Sounds a Warning--Exclusive Interview." *U.S. News and World Report*, 19 May 1969, 40-44.

"Democracy's Survival Problematic." *Antioch College Record*, 23 May 1969, 6.

"The Barbarism of Virtue." *PMLA* 84 (May 1969): 465-75.
[Reprinted in **Academic Freedom and Academic Anarchy**, 1970.]

"*Modern Quarterly*, A Chapter in American Radical History: V. F. Calverton and His Periodicals." *Labor History* 10 (Spring 1969): 241-49.

"Labor Sit-Ins and University Sit-Ins: The Crucial Differences." *Measure* no. 2 (June 1969): 5.

"John Dewey and the Crisis of American Liberalism." *Antioch Review* 29 (Summer 1969): 218-32.

"The Crisis of Our Democratic Institutions." *Humanist* 29 (July-Aug. 1969): 6-7.

"Why *Not* Shut It Down?" *Measure* no. 3 (Sept. 1969): 5.

"The Architecture of Educational Chaos." *Phi Delta Kappan* 51 (Oct. 1969): 68-70.
>Response to Harold Taylor, "The Student Revolution." Ibid., 62-67.
>Comments by Harold Taylor, "Students, Universities, and Sidney Hook." Ibid. 51 (Dec. 1969): 195-97.
>Response by Hook, "Harold Taylor's Evasions." Ibid., 197-98.

Review of **The Sociology of Marx**, by Henri Lefebvre. Translated from French by Norbert Guterman. *American Historical Review* 75 (Oct. 1969): 148-49.

"The Poisoned Premise of Campus Disruption." *Measure* no. 5 (Nov. 1969): 5.

1970

Academic Freedom and Academic Anarchy. New York: Cowles Book Co., 1970.
[Reviewed in *AAUP Bulletin* 56 (Sept. 1970): 334-35 (O. Lawrence Burnette, Jr.); *Booklist* 66 (15 May 1970): 1124; *Choice* 7 (Sept. 1970): 906; *Christian Century* 87 (7 Jan. 1970): 22; *Christian Science Monitor*, 22 Oct. 1970, 9 (C. Michael Curtis); *College and University Business* 48 (May 1970): 16; *Humanist* 30 (May-June 1970): 42 (Edward Chalfant); ibid., 42-43 (Gordon W. Keller); *Kirkus* 37 (1 Nov. 1969): 183; *Library Journal* 95 (1 Jan. 1970): 57 (Henry J. Steck); *Minnesota Law Review* 55 (June 1971): 1275-85 (Nelson W. Polsby); *Modern Age* 15 (Winter 1971): 96-99 (C. P. Ives); *National Review* 22 (27 Jan. 1970): 91-92 (Russell Kirk); *New York Review of Books* 14 (12 Feb. 1970): 5-11 (Henry David Aiken); *New York Times Book Review*, 8 Mar. 1970, 25-29 (Edgar Z. Friedenberg); *Philosophy Forum* Supp. (De Kalb) 11 (Summer 1972): S77-S82 (Paul Kurtz); ibid., S82-S87 (Gail Kennedy); *Publishers Weekly* 196 (27 Oct. 1969): 57-58; *Quarterly Journal of Speech* 56 (Dec. 1970): 451-52 (Malcolm O. Sillars); *Review for Religious* 29 (May 1970): 483-84 (Vernon J. Bourke); *Saturday Review* 53 (24 Jan. 1970): 67-68 (Lewis B. Mayhew).]

"Paradise Lost: The Tragedy of Whittaker Chambers." Review of **Odyssey of a Friend: Whittaker Chambers' Letters to William F. Buckley, Jr., 1954-1961**, by Whittaker Chambers. *Chicago Sun-Times Book Week*,

1 Feb. 1970, 3.

Letter. *Measure* no. 6 (Jan. 1970): 5.
> Reply to Everett E. Hagen, ibid.
> Comment by Oscar Handlin, ibid.

"The Challenge to Professional Ethics." *Measure* no. 7 (Mar. 1970): 1-2.

"Conflict and Change in the Academic Community." In **Papers of the Fifty-second Annual Conference**, National Association of Student Personnel Administrators, 1-4 Apr. 1970, 5-14.

"Friedenberg." *New York Times Book Review*, 5 Apr. 1970, 28.
> Reply to Edgar Z. Friedenberg's review of **Academic Freedom and Academic Anarchy**. Ibid., 8 Mar. 1970, 25-29.
> Comments by Jay Schulman, Richard Gambino, Robert B. Sutton, and April Oursler Armstrong, ibid., 5 Apr. 1970, 28-29.

"Justice Douglas." Letter to the editor. *New York Times*, 19 Apr. 1970, 17.

"The Ideology of Violence." *Encounter* 34 (Apr. 1970): 26-29, 31-38.

"What Student Rights in Education?" *Current* no. 117 (Apr. 1970): 21-27.

"Philosophy and Public Policy." *Journal of Philosophy* 67 (23 July 1970): 461-70.
[Reprinted in **Philosophy and Public Policy**, 1980.]

"A Plan to Achieve Campus Peace." *Los Angeles Times*, 30 Aug. 1970, sec. F, 7.

"From the Platitudinous to the Absurd." *Philosophic Exchange* 1 (Summer 1970): 21-30.
> Reply to Henry David Aiken, "Can American Universities be Depoliticized?" Ibid., 3-19.
[Reprinted in **In Defense of Academic Freedom**, 1971.]

"Hook's Views on Riots." *New York Times*, 30 Sept. 1970, 42.

"Points of Confusion." Review of **Points of Rebellion**, by William O. Douglas. *Encounter* 35 (Sept. 1970): 45-53.

"The Survival of the Free University." *Humanist* 30 (Sept.-Oct. 1970): 26-28.

Contribution to "Forum: Points of Rebellion." A Brooklyn Law School

symposium on **Points of Rebellion**, by William O. Douglas. *Brooklyn Law Review* 37 (Fall 1970): 16-22.
> Panel Discussion, ibid., 22-32.

"Law and Anarchy." *University of Richmond Law Review* 5 (Fall 1970): 47-69.
[Reprinted in **Philosophy and Public Policy**, 1980.]

"Corporate Politics on Campus." *Freedom at Issue* 3 (Sept.-Oct. 1970): 11-13.

"Campus Terror: An Indictment." *New York Times*, 22 Oct. 1970, 47.
> Reply by Lipman Bers, ibid., 30 Oct. 1970, 40.

"The Politicalized Scotch." Letter to Bernard Goldberg. *Measure* no. 10 (Nov. 1970): 5.

"The Political Fantasies of Noam Chomsky." *Humanist* 30 (Nov.-Dec. 1970): 26-29.
> Reply to Noam Chomsky, "The Student Movement." Ibid. 30 (Sept.-Oct. 1970): 19-25.
> Response by Chomsky, ibid. 31 (Jan.-Feb. 1971): 23-29.
> Reply by Hook, "The Knight of the Double Standard." Ibid., 29-34.
> Response by Chomsky, "Response to Sidney Hook II." Ibid. 31 (Mar.-Apr. 1971): 30-34.
> Reply by Hook, "The Knight Comes a Cropper." Ibid., 34-35.

1971

In Defense of Academic Freedom, edited by Sidney Hook. New York: Pegasus, 1971.
[Reviewed in *Choice* 8 (Sept. 1971): 880; *Journal of Higher Education* 43 (Feb. 1972): 162-63 (Phillip Monypenny); *Library Journal* 96 (1 Nov. 1971): 3604 (James Ranz).]

"Preface," "The Long View," "Conflict and Change in the Academic Community," and "From the Platitudinous to the Absurd." In **In Defense of Academic Freedom**, edited by Sidney Hook, v, 11-20, 106-19, 249-66. New York: Pegasus, 1971.

"Academic Freedom and the Supreme Court: The Court in Another Wilderness." In **On Academic Freedom**, edited by Valerie Earle, 31-46. Washington, D.C.: American Enterprise Institute for Public Policy Research, 1971.

"How Democratic Is America? A Response to Howard Zinn." In **How Democratic Is America? Responses to the New Left Challenge**, edited by Robert A. Goldwin, 61-75. Chicago: Rand McNally and Co., 1971.

"Ideals and Realities of Academic Tenure." In **Twenty-eighth Annual Utah Conference on Higher Education**, 13-24. Logan: Utah State University, 1971.

"Ideologies of Violence and Social Change." In **Peaceful Change in Modern Society**, edited by E. Berkeley Tompkins, 112-27, 157-58. Stanford, Calif.: Leland Stanford Junior University, 1971.
[Reprinted in **Revolution, Reform, and Social Justice**, 1975.]

"A Sentimental View of Crime." Review of **Crime in America**, by Ramsey Clark. *Fortune* 83 (Feb. 1971): 140-41.

"Academic Freedom and Faculty Disruption." *Measure* no. 12 (Mar. 1971): 3-4.

"Comments on Professor Nelson's Address." *Personalist* 52 (Spring 1971): 335-42.
     Comments on John O. Nelson, "The Function of Government." Ibid., 161-85.

"The Snare of Definitions." *Humanist* 31 (Sept.-Oct. 1971): 10-11.

"The Cult of Revolution." *Quadrant* 15 (Sept.-Oct. 1971): 51-64.

"An American Verdict on Star-Spangled Australia." *Sunday Australian*, 31 Oct. 1971, 10.

"Discrimination, Color Blindness and the Quota System." *Measure* no. 14 (Oct. 1971): 3-4.
     Reply by Milton Friedman, ibid. 16 (Jan. 1972): 4-5.
     Response by Hook, ibid.

"Discrimination against the Qualified?" *New York Times*, 5 Nov. 1971, 43.
     Reply by Martha Burke-Hennessy and Myra L. Skluth, "University Bias." Ibid., 24 Nov. 1971, 34.
     Response by J. Stanley Pottinger, "Come Now, Professor Hook." Ibid., 18 Dec. 1971, 29.
     Response by Frank Askin, "Bias Against Blacks." Ibid., 19 Dec. 1971, 10.

"John Dewey and His Betrayers." **Papers on Educational Reform**, vol. 2 (La Salle, Ill.: Open Court Publishing Co., 1971): 111-33; *Change* 3 (Nov.

1971): 22-26.
> Comment by Albert Shanker, "The Educational 'Progressives': A New Establishment." *New York Times*, 3 Oct. 1971, 9.
> Response by Frederick L. Redefer, *Change* 4 (Feb. 1972): 4-5.
> Response by Preston Greene, ibid., 5.
> Reply by Hook, ibid.

"Authority and Democracy in the University." *Quadrant* 15 (Nov.-Dec. 1971): 42-48.

"Epilogue: Democracy and the Open Society." Contribution to a forum on New Directions for America. *Humanist* 31 (Nov.-Dec. 1971): 29-31.

"HEW Regionals--A New Threat to Educational Integrity." *Freedom at Issue* no. 10 (Nov.-Dec. 1971): 5-7.

1972

Introduction to **Contemporary Problems of Democracy**, by Marvin Zimmerman, ix-xiv. New York: Humanities Press, 1972.

"The Freedom Shouters." Letter by Hook and Miro Todorovich. *New York Times*, 17 Jan. 1972, 30.
> Reply to Richard D. Lyons, "Critical Scientists Less Rowdy." Ibid., 29 Dec. 1971, 18.
> Reply by Barry Commoner, "Dissension vs. Disruption." Ibid., 28 Jan. 1972, 44.

Introduction to "Civil Disobedience," by Ernest van den Haag. *National Review* 24 (21 Jan. 1972): 29.

"Illich's De-Schooled Utopia." Review of **De-schooling Society**, by Ivan Illich. *Encounter* 38 (Jan. 1972): 53-57.
> Reply by James Wellard, "Illich's 'Gimmick.'" Ibid. 38 (Apr. 1972): 93.
> Response by Hook, ibid.
> [Reprinted in **Education and the Taming of Power**, 1973.]

"Democracy and Genetic Variation." *Humanist* 32 (Mar.-Apr. 1972): 7.

"Force Faculty 'Quotas'--HEW: The Road to a University 'Quota System.'" *Freedom at Issue* no. 12 (Mar.-Apr. 1972): 1-2, 21-22.
> Response by Jack Hirshleifer, ibid., 23.
> Reply by Hook, "HEW's Faculty 'Quotas' Inspire Semantic Eva-

sions." Ibid. no. 14 (July-Aug. 1972): 12-14.
Comment by Hook et al., "Quotas in the Universities." *Humanist* 32 (Nov.-Dec. 1972): 45.

"The Rights of the Victims." *Encounter* 38 (Apr. 1972): 11-15.
Editorial response, "Crime and Its Victims." *Wall Street Journal*, 11 Apr. 1972, 22.

"Adrienne Koch: Student and Colleague." *Maryland Historian* 3 (Spring 1972): 5-8.

"Repression in Yugoslavia." Letter by Hook et al. *Humanist* 32 (July-Aug. 1972): 2.

"Author's Response." *Philosophy Forum* Supp. (DeKalb) 11 (Summer 1972): S88-S95.
Response to Paul Kurtz's and Gail Kennedy's reviews of **Academic Freedom and Academic Anarchy.** Ibid., S77-S87.

"To the Editor of *Lithopinion*." *Lithopinion* 7 (Summer 1972): 14.
Reply to Fred J. Cook, "Memo to Vice President Spiro T. Agnew: 'There is no Eastern Intellectual Elite; there is no Eastern Liberal Press.'" Ibid., 8-13.

"A Democratic Socialist Tells Why He's for Nixon." *Los Angeles Times*, 19 Oct. 1972, pt. 2, 7.

"Uncertain Progress." *Measure* no. 20 (Oct. 1972): 1-2.

"The Promise and Confusion of American Education." *Quadrant* 16 (Nov.-Dec. 1972): 81-87.

Letter to the editor. Letter by Hook, Paul Seabury, and Miro M. Todorovich. *Newsweek*, 25 Dec. 1972, 5.
Response to Jerrold K. Footlick, "Faculty Backlash." Ibid., 4 Dec. 1972, 127-28.

1973

Education and the Taming of Power. La Salle, Ill.: Open Court Publishing Co., 1973.
[Reviewed in *AAUP Bulletin* 61 (Oct. 1975): 248-51 (Ronald M. Johnson); *American School Board Journal* 161 (Dec. 1974): 49-50; *Change* 6 (Apr. 1974): 58-60 (John K. Jessup); *Childhood Education* 51 (Apr.-May 1975): 332 (Beth H. Griesel); *Chronicle of Higher Education* 8

(19 Feb. 1974): 9-10 (Paul Lauter); *Educational Studies* 5 (Winter 1974-75): 246-47 (Richard Gambino); *Education Digest* 39 (Feb. 1974): 70; *Journal of Education* (Boston Univ.) 156 (Nov. 1974): 74-75 (Gene D. Phillips); *Library Journal* 98 (15 Nov. 1973): 3373 (Adeline Konsh); *Modern Age* 19 (Fall 1975): 423-25 (Hugh Mercer Curtler); *National Review* 26 (30 Aug. 1974): 992 (Aram Bakshian, Jr.); *New Republic* 170 (9 Feb. 1974): 30 (Joseph Featherstone); *News from Open Court*, 25 Nov. 1973, 29-30; *Review of Education* 1 (May 1975): 298-302 (Terry Nichols Clark and Priscilla P. Clark); *Saturday Review/World* 1 (27 July 1974): 52 (John Calam); *Times Educational Supplement*, 10 May 1974, 24 (R. S. Peters).]

Education for Modern Man: A New Perspective. Enl. ed. Atlantic Highlands, N. J.: Humanities Press, 1973.

Heresy, Yes--Conspiracy, No. With new introduction. Westport, Conn.: Greenwood Press, 1973.

Foreword to **Radical School Reform, Critique and Alternatives**, edited by Cornelius J. Troost, vii-xiii. Boston: Little, Brown and Co., 1973.

"Marxism." In **Dictionary of the History of Ideas**, edited by Philip P. Wiener, vol. 3, 146-61. New York: Charles Scribner's Sons, 1973.

"The Relevance of John Dewey's Thought." In **The Chief Glory of Every People**, edited by Matthew Bruccoli, 53-75. Carbondale: Southern Illinois University Press, 1973.

"Lenin and the Communist International." Review of **Lenin and the Comintern**, by Branko Lazitch and Milorad M. Drachkovitch, vol. 1. *Russian Review* 32 (Jan. 1973): 1-14.
[Reprinted in **Marxism and Beyond**, 1983.]

"Reaction to Miles." *Change* 5 (Feb. 1973): 10.
    Response to Michael Miles, "The Triumph of Reaction." Ibid. 4 (Winter 1972-73): 30-36.
    Response by Miles, ibid. 5 (Feb. 1973): 10.

"'Conservatism: New Attention . . . .'" *Los Angeles Times*, 28 Mar. 1973, Part II, 6.
    Reply to Robert Shogan, "Conservatism: New Attention, New Respect." Ibid., 15 Mar. 1973, 1, 14-15.

"The Politics of Irresponsibility." Review of **The Party of Eros: Radical Social Thought and the Realm of Freedom**, by Richard King. *Virginia*

Quarterly Review 49 (Spring 1973): 274-82.

"Make the Punishment Fit the Criminal." *New York Times*, 6 Apr. 1973, 40.
Response by Mary Ellen Travis, "To Protect the People." Ibid., 19
Apr. 1973, 42.

"The Academic Mission and Collective Bargaining." In **Proceedings of the
First Annual Conference**, National Center for the Study of Collective
Bargaining in Higher Education, New York City, Apr. 1973, 8-17.

"Myth and Fact in the Marxist Theory of Revolution and Violence."
Journal of the History of Ideas 34 (Apr.-June 1973): 271-80.
[Reprinted in **Revolution, Reform, and Social Justice**, 1975, and
Marxism and Beyond, 1983.]

"Semantics and Politics." *Measure* no. 23 (May 1973): 1-2.

"Solzhenitsyn and the Western Liberals." *New York Times*, 19 Sept. 1973,
46.
Reply to Theodore Shabad, "Solzhenitsyn Assails Liberals in West."
Ibid., 12 Sept. 1973, 3.
Reply by John V. Wells, "Communism, Capitalism and the Liberal
Cause." Ibid., 29 Sept. 1973, 30.

"John Reed, the Romantic." Review of **So Short a Time**, by Barbara Gelb.
New Republic 169 (29 Sept. 1973): 23-25.

"Have We Reached Shore?" *Measure* no. 24 (Sept. 1973): 1-3.

"Humanist Manifesto II." Sidney Hook et al. *Humanist* 33 (Sept.-Oct.
1973): 4-9.

"Materials for a Biography." Review of **The Life and Mind of John Dewey**,
by George Dykhuizen. *New Republic* 169 (27 Oct. 1973): 38-39.

"For Louis Althusser." Review of **For Marx**, by Louis Althusser.
Encounter 41 (Oct. 1973): 86-92.

"William James and George Santayana." *ICarbS* 1 (Fall-Winter 1973): 34-
39.

"Professing the Truth: An Exchange." With Martin Duberman,
Christopher Lasch, Lionel Tiger, Arthur C. Danto, René Wellek, Dennis
H. Wrong, and George Gibian. *Columbia Forum* 2 (Winter 1973): 38-46.
Reply to Robert Gorham Davis, "The Professors' Lie." Ibid. 1 (Fall
1972): 6-15.

Response by Davis, ibid. 2 (Winter 1973): 46-49, 57.

"The Attack on Objectivity." *Measure* no. 26 (Dec. 1973): 1-2.

1974

Pragmatism and the Tragic Sense of Life. New York: Basic Books, 1974.
[Reviewed in *Commentary* 59 (June 1975): 86, 88 (Michael Novak);
Encounter 45 (Oct. 1975): 37-45 (Lewis S. Feuer); *Humanist* 35 (July-
Aug. 1975): 39 (Steven M. Cahn); *Journal of the History of Ideas* 36
(Oct.-Dec. 1975): 739-46 (Philip P. Wiener); *Journal of Philosophy* 74
(Mar. 1977): 172-76 (Frederick A. Olafson); *Library Journal* 100 (15 Feb.
1975): 396 (Robert Hoffman); *Midstream* 21 (Dec. 1975): 70 (Reuben
Abel); *National Review* 28 (23 Jan. 1976): 44-46 (Frederick L. Will); *New
Republic* 175 (18 Sept. 1976): 35-37 (William K. Frankena); *Philosophy
and Phenomenological Research* 36 (Dec. 1975): 275-77 (Henry W.
Johnstone, Jr.); *Review for Religious* 34 (May 1975): 491 (Patrick Henry
Reardon); *St. Croix Review* 8 (June 1975): 48; *Virginia Quarterly Review*
51 (Summer 1975): cxxvi; *Wall Street Journal*, 4 Feb. 1975, 20 (Edmund
Fuller).]

The Idea of a Modern University, edited by Sidney Hook, Paul Kurtz, and
Miro Todorovich. Buffalo, N.Y.: Prometheus Books, 1974.
[Reviewed in *Bibliographie de la Philosophie* 22 (1975): 243-44 (Loy
Littlefield); *Change* 6 (Sept. 1974): 56-57 (Sol Cohen); *Choice* 11 (Nov.
1974): 1362; *Commonweal* 101 (4 Oct. 1974): 18, 20-22 (Dennis
O'Brien); *Educational Studies* 6 (Fall-Winter 1975): 217-18 (Milton K.
Reimer); *Humanist* 35 (Mar.-Apr. 1975): 33-35 (David Sidorsky); *Inter-
national Philosophical Quarterly* 16 (June 1976): 248-51 (John Donnelly);
Journal of General Education 27 (Summer 1975): 160-64 (Daniel
Walden); *Library Journal* 99 (Aug. 1974): 1944 (Adeline Konsh); *Review
of Education* 1 (May 1975): 298-302 (Terry Nichols Clark and Priscilla P.
Clark).]

"Introduction: The Rationale of the Problem" and "Democracy and Higher
Education." In **The Idea of a Modern University**, edited by Sidney
Hook, Paul Kurtz, and Miro Todorovich, xvii-xix, 33-40. Buffalo, N.Y.:
Prometheus Books, 1974.

"The Modern Quarterly: Baltimore and New York, 1923-1932, 1938-1940.
The Modern Monthly: New York, 1933-1938." In **The American Radi-
cal Press**, vol. 2, edited by Joseph R. Conlin, 596-605. Westport, Conn.:
Greenwood Press, 1974.

"Reflections on the Disorder of Our Times." *Papers on Educational Reform*

4 (1974): 117-28; *Alternative* 7 (Jan. 1974): 5-7.

"Humanism and the Human Experience." *Humanist* 34 (Jan.-Feb. 1974): 6-7.
> Reply to Garry Wills, "Critique of the Humanist Manifesto." Ibid., 6.

"American Group Defended." *Times Higher Education Supplement*, 15 Feb. 1974, 12.
> Reply to Angela Stent, "Faculty Lines Forming Against 'The Enemy Within.'" Ibid., 14 Dec. 1973, 11.

"Violence Usually Frustrates or Delays Reform." *Los Angeles Times*, 27 Feb. 1974, 7.

"Letter from New York: Dangerous Doubts." *Encounter* 42 (Feb. 1974): 44-45.

Letter to the editor. *Chronicle of Higher Education* 8 (18 Mar. 1974): 8.
> Reply to Paul Lauter's review of **Education and the Taming of Power.** Ibid. 8 (19 Feb. 1974): 9-10.

"Anyone for Objectivity?" *Encounter* 42 (Mar. 1974): 94-95.

"The Education of an Autodidact." Review of **Hoffer's America**, by James D. Koerner. *Change* 6 (Mar. 1974): 60-61.

"John Dewey's **Democracy and Education.**" *New York University Education Quarterly* 5 (Spring 1974): 26-29.

"Stalin--Mystery and Legacy." Review of **Joseph Stalin: Man and Legend,** by Ronald Hingley; **Stalin as Revolutionary,** by Robert C. Tucker; and **Stalin: The Man and His Era,** by Adam B. Ulam. *New Republic* 171 (20 July 1974): 21-24.

"The Bias in Anti-Bias Regulations." *Measure* no. 30 (Summer 1974): 1-2, 4-6.

"Congressional Testimony: On Discrimination." *Measure* no. 31 (Sept. 1974): 1-2, 5-6.
> Reply by Laurence Hyman, ibid. 33 (Feb. 1975): 3.
> Rejoinder by Miro Todorovich, ibid., 3-4.

"A Quota Is a Quota Is a Quota." *New York Times*, 12 Nov. 1974, 39.
> Reply by Peter J. Wilson, ibid., 27 Nov. 1974, 36.

Reply by Nancy Alderman Ransom, ibid., 2 Dec. 1974, 32.
Comments by James Cass, *Saturday Review*, 8 Feb. 1975, 45.

"Will to Illusion." Review of **An Opposing Man**, by Ernst Fisher. *New Republic* 171 (16 Nov. 1974): 27-28.

"A Bolshevik Reconsidered: The Case of Comrade Bukharin." Review of **Bukharin and the Bolshevik Revolution, 1888-1938**, by Stephen F. Cohen. *Encounter* 43 (Dec. 1974): 81-92.
[Reprinted in **Revolution, Reform, and Social Justice**, 1975.]

"Ill-Tempered Review." *Change* 6 (Dec.-Jan. 1974-75): 4.
Reply to Sol Cohen's review of **The Idea of a Modern University**. Ibid. 6 (Sept. 1974): 56-57.
Response by Cohen, ibid. 6 (Dec.-Jan. 1974-75): 4.

1975

Revolution, Reform, and Social Justice--Studies in the Theory and Practice of Marxism. New York: New York University Press, 1975.
[Reviewed in *Choice* 13 (Mar. 1976): 104; *Economist* 262 (8 Jan. 1977): 101-2; *Humanist* 36 (May-June 1976): 36-37 (Marvin Kohl); *International Studies in Philosophy* 9 (1977): 193-95 (Donald Weiss); *Journal of Economic Issues* 11 (Dec. 1977): 904-6 (Howard Sherman); *New Republic* 174 (14 Feb. 1976): 24-25 (Irving Howe); *Political Studies* 25 (Dec. 1977): 629 (David Miller); *Review of Education* 3 (Jan.-Feb. 1977): 71-76 (Brian Hendley); *Review of Metaphysics* 29 (June 1976): 737-38 (Michael P. Malloy); *Sociology* 12 (Jan. 1978): 180-81 (Peter Lassman); *Sovetskoe Gosudarstro: Pravo* (USSR) 48 (May 1978): 98-100 (G. V. Mal'tsev); *Studi internazionali di filosofia* 9 (1977): 193-95 (Donald Weiss); *Studies in Soviet Thought* 24 (Nov. 1982): 295-98 (Thomas A. Shipka); *Times* (London) *Literary Supplement*, 8 Apr. 1977, 427 (Ghita Ionescu).]

The Philosophy of the Curriculum: The Need for General Education, edited by Sidney Hook, Paul Kurtz, and Miro Todorovich. Buffalo, N.Y.: Prometheus Books, 1975.
[Reviewed in *Change* 7 (Sept. 1975): 58-59 (Maurice Hungiville); *Choice* 12 (Nov. 1975): 1215; *Chronicle of Higher Education* 14 (11 Oct. 1976): 17 (Leon Botstein); *College and University* 52 (Winter 1977): 240 (Robert A. Scott); *Encounter* 45 (Oct. 1975): 37; *Higher Education* (Netherlands) 5 (Aug. 1976): 349-50 (Samuel E. Kellams); *Humanist* 35 (Nov.-Dec. 1975): 38-39 (Robert Simon).]

"Introduction," "General Education: The Minimum Indispensables," and "On Sharpening the Horns." In **The Philosophy of the Curriculum: The**

Need for General Education, edited by Sidney Hook, Paul Kurtz, and Miro Todorovich, xi-xiii, 27-36, 211-15. Buffalo, N.Y.: Prometheus Books, 1975.

Preface to **Moral Principles in Education**, by John Dewey, vii-xvi. Carbondale and Edwardsville: Southern Illinois University Press, Arcturus Books, 1975.

"For An Open Minded Naturalism." *Southern Journal of Philosophy* 13 (1975): 127-36.

"In the Forefront." *New York Post*, 1 Feb. 1975, 26.
     Response to Carl Rowan, "The War on Quotas." Ibid., 20 Jan. 1975, 2.
[Complete letter printed in *Measure* no. 33 (Feb. 1975): 6.]

"Education: The Wrong Affirmative Action." Letter by Sidney Hook et al. *New York Times*, 29 Mar. 1975, 22.

"What the Cold War Was About." *Encounter* 44 (Mar. 1975): 62-67; *Freedom at Issue* no. 30 (Mar.-Apr. 1975): 4-6; *Quest* 96 (July-Aug. 1975): 55-58.
     Reply by Henry M. Pachter, *Freedom at Issue* no. 31 (May-June 1975): 17-18.
     Response by Hook, ibid., 18-19.

"'Not Good' Is Not Enough." Statement by Hook et al. *Freedom at Issue* no. 30 (Mar.-Apr. 1975): 2-3.

"A Humanist Philosophy of Life." Review of **The Fullness of Life**, by Paul Kurtz. *Humanist* 35 (Mar.-Apr. 1975): 36-37.

"University Women: An Exchange." *New York Review of Books* 22 (3 Apr. 1975): 36-37.
     Reply by Gertrude Ezorsky, ibid., 37-38.

"America Now: A Failure of Nerve?--A Symposium." *Commentary* 60 (July 1975): 41-43.

"The Hiss Ruling's Contradictions." *Wall Street Journal*, 25 Aug. 1975, 6.
     Response by John F. Burke, ibid., 29 Sept. 1975, 11.
     Reply by Hook, ibid.

"The Promise of Humanism." *Humanist* 35 (Sept.-Oct. 1975): 41-43.
     Response to Jerome D. Frank, "The Limits of Humanism." Ibid., 38-40.

Reply by Albert Ellis, "Comments on Frank's 'The Limits of Human-
ism.'" Ibid., 43-45.
Response by Frank, ibid. 35 (Nov.-Dec. 1975): 34.
Rejoinder by Hook, ibid., 34-35.

"In Defense of Terminological Sobriety: A Reply to Professor Kellner."
Journal of Politics 37 (Nov. 1975): 912-16.
Reply to Menachem Marc Kellner, "Democracy and Civil Dis-
obedience." Ibid., 899-911.

"The Tyranny of Reverse Discrimination." With Miro Todorovich. *Change*
7 (Dec. 1975-Jan. 1976): 42-43.

1976

**Ethics, National Ideology, Marxism and Existentialism: Discussions with
Sidney Hook**. Edited by Harsja W. Bachtiar. Jakarta, Indonesia: Djam-
batan, 1976. In Indonesian and English.

Foreword to **The Moral Writings of John Dewey**, by James Gouinlock, ix-xi.
New York: Macmillan Co., Hafner Press, 1976.

Introduction to **The Middle Works of John Dewey, 1899-1924**, edited by Jo
Ann Boydston, vol. 2, ix-xxi. Carbondale and Edwardsville: Southern
Illinois University Press, 1976.

"Higher Education and Morality." In American Association of Presidents
of Independent Colleges and Universities Annual Meeting Talks, vol. 4,
Private Higher Education: The Job Ahead, 21-26, Scottsdale, Ariz.,
1975. Malibu, Calif.: AAPICU, 1976.

"The Strange Case of Whittaker Chambers." *Encounter* 46 (Jan. 1976): 78-
89.

Review of **Up from Communism**, by John Patrick Diggins. *New Republic*
174 (21 Feb. 1976): 24-27.
Reply by Diggins, ibid. 174 (12 June 1976): 31-32.
Response by Hook, ibid., 32.

"Alger Hiss: The Continuing Whitewash." Review of **Alger Hiss: The True
Story**, by John Chabot Smith. *Wall Street Journal*, 22 Mar. 1976, 14.

"Intelligence, Morality and Foreign Policy." *Freedom at Issue* no. 35 (Mar.-
Apr. 1976): 3-6; *New York Times*, 1 May 1976, 23.
[Reprinted in **Philosophy and Public Policy**, 1980.]

"The Legacy of 1776--and a New Call for Freedom." *American Views* 1 (5 July 1976): 1-2.

"Bertrand Russell the Man." *Commentary* 62 (July 1976): 52-54.

Review of **The Twilight of Capitalism: A Marxian Epitaph**, by Michael Harrington. *New Republic* 175 (7 and 14 Aug. 1976): 34-37. [Reprinted in **Marxism and Beyond**, 1983.]

"Morris Cohen--Fifty Years Later." *American Scholar* 45 (Summer 1976): 426-36.
  Reply by Mortimer Smith, ibid. 46 (Winter 1976-77): 142.
  Response by Hook, ibid., 142-43.

"The Social Democratic Prospect." *New America* 13 (Aug.-Sept. 1976): 8-9, 14-15.
[Reprinted in **Philosophy and Public Policy**, 1980.]

"The Big Casino in the Sky." *New York Times*, 3 Sept. 1976, A19.

"It's All in the Cards, My Dear. (Luck plays important role in life.)" *Fort Worth Star-Telegram*, 19 Sept. 1976.

"Can the University Survive Equal Access?" Review of **On the Meaning of the University**, edited by Sterling M. McMurrin. *Change* 8 (Sept. 1976): 59-61.

"A Symposium: What Is a Liberal--Who Is a Conservative?" *Commentary* 62 (Sept. 1976): 69-70.

"Is Secular Humanism a Religion?" *Humanist* 36 (Sept.-Oct. 1976): 5-7.

"The Meaning of Freedom." The Fourth Sol Feinstone Lecture. United States Military Academy. West Point, New York, 3 Nov. 1976, 12 pp. [Reprinted in **Marxism and Beyond**, 1983.]

Review of **My Country and the World**, by Andrei D. Sakharov. *Russian Review* 35 (Oct. 1976): 486-87.

"A Voice from Another Shore." Review of **The Education of Lev Navrozov**, by Lev Navrozov. *Humanist* 36 (Nov.-Dec. 1976): 47, 50.

"An Interview with Sidney Hook." *Forum* (Austin, Tex.) 1 (Dec. 1976): 6-7.

"Letters from George Santayana." *American Scholar* 46 (Winter 1976-77): 76.

1977

The Ethics of Teaching and Scientific Research, edited by Sidney Hook,
Paul Kurtz, and Miro Todorovich. Buffalo, N.Y.: Prometheus Books,
1977.
[Reviewed in *Contemporary Psychology* 23 (May 1978): 371 (Dennis T.
Regan); *Higher Education* 7 (Aug. 1978): 375-76 (David Nyberg);
National Association of Secondary School Principals Bulletin 62 (Mar.
1978): 114 (Weldon Beckner); *New Scientist* 75 (7 July 1977): 30 (Tim
Robinson); *Religious Studies Review* 7 (Jan. 1981): 53 (Hans O. Tiefel);
Review of Metaphysics 31 (Dec. 1977): 320 (Milton Goldinger); *Science
Books and Films* 13 (Mar. 1978): 197 (Rachelle D. Hollander).]

"Introduction," "Academic Freedom and Professional Responsibilities,"
and "Dr. Hibbs and the Ethics of Discussion." In **The Ethics of Teaching and Scientific Research**, edited by Sidney Hook, Paul Kurtz, and
Miro Todorovich, xi-xiii, 117-23, 187-90. Buffalo, N.Y.: Prometheus
Books, 1977.

"The New Religiosity." Part of a symposium entitled "The Resurgence of
Fundamentalism." *Humanist* 37 (Jan.-Feb. 1977): 38-39.

"Lillian Hellman's *Scoundrel Time*." Review of **Scoundrel Time**, by Lillian
Hellman. *Encounter* 48 (Feb. 1977): 82-91.
Reply by Patrick J. Buchanan, "Ex-Stalinist Lillian Toast of Chic
Bash." *Times-Picayune* (New Orleans, La.), 23 Nov. 1977, Sec. 1,
12.

"Racial & Sexual Quotas: They're Not Only Illegal: They're Immoral."
New York Daily News, 27 Mar. 1977, 64.

"To Teach the Truth without Let or Hindrance." *Chronicle of Higher
Education* 14 (4 Apr. 1977): 40.
Reply by Leonard Marsak, ibid. 14 (2 May 1977): 16.
Response by Hook, ibid. 14 (23 May 1977): 11.

"Marxists and Non-Marxists." *Times Literary Supplement* 88 (29 Apr. 1977):
522.
Reply to Ghita Ionescu's review of **Revolution, Reform, and Social
Justice**, ibid., 427.

"An Outstanding Symbol of Free Trade Unions." *New America* 14 (May
1977): 8.

"Fanaticism and Absolutism." *Intellect* 105 (May 1977): 387-88.

"Challenge from a Social Democrat: An Interview with Sidney Hook."
Interview by Tibor R. Machan and Davis Keeler. *Reason* 9 (May 1977):
28-34.

"Marxism and Crypto-Marxism." *New York Times*, 26 Oct. 1977, 27; *San
Francisco Chronicle*, 26 Nov. 1977, 32.
　　Reply by Harry Binswanger, "Invisible Freedom." *New York Times*,
　　11 Nov. 1977, 28.

"The Bias in Public Media Programs." *Measure* no. 44 (Oct. 1977): 3-5.

"Socialism Means Freedom." Interview with Hook. *New America* 14 (Oct.
1977): 9-10; ibid. 14 (Nov. 1977): 8.

"Reflections on the Metaphysics of John Dewey: **Experience and Nature.**"
*Revue Internationale de Philosophie (La Pensée Philosophique
Américaine, 1776-1976)* no. 121-22 (1977): 313-28.

1978

**The University and the State: What Role for Government in Higher
Education?** edited by Sidney Hook, Paul Kurtz, and Miro Todorovich.
Buffalo, N.Y.: Prometheus Books, 1978.
[Reviewed in *Booklist* 75 (1 Sept. 1978): 6; *Change* 10 (Oct. 1978): 60
(Joseph Barbato); *Choice* 15 (Dec. 1978): 1419; *Educational Studies* 11
(Spring 1980): 77-80 (M. M. Chambers); *Inquiry* 2 (8 and 22 Jan. 1979):
25-26 (Joseph R. Peden); *Journal of Church and State* 22 (Autumn
1980): 540-41 (Timothy J. Hansen); *Journal of Higher Education* 51
(Sept.-Oct. 1980): 569-72 (Jerry A. May); *Journal of Politics* 41 (Aug.
1979): 1010-11 (Glenn E. Brooks); *Library Journal* 103 (Aug. 1978):
1505-6 (Carol Eckberg Wadsworth); *National Forum* 59 (Summer 1979):
43 (James T. Hamilton); *New England Law Review* 14 (Summer 1978):
144-45; *Perspective* 8 (Jan.-Feb. 1979): 5 (Norman Lederer); *Publishers
Weekly* 214 (3 July 1978): 56.]

The Hero in History: Myth, Power, or Moral Ideal? Hoover Institution on
War, Revolution and Peace, 15 pp. Stanford University, 1978.
[Reprinted in **Philosophy and Public Policy**, 1980.]

"Bernstein's Contribution to Social Democracy." *New America* 15 (Jan.
1978): 2, 8.

"Of I.Q. Tests and the Desire to Succeed." Letter to the editor. *New York
Times*, 3 Mar. 1978, 24.
　　Reply to George W. Albee, "I.Q. Tests on Trial." Ibid., 12 Feb.

1978, 13.

"Bert Brecht, Sidney Hook, & Stalin." *Encounter* 50 (Mar. 1978): 93.
 Reply to Martin Esslin's "Icon & Self-Portrait: Images of Brecht."
 Ibid. 49 (Dec. 1977): 30-39.
 Reply by Esslin, "Hook and Brecht, & Stalin." Ibid. 50 (Apr.
 1978): 90.
 Comment by J. B. Phillips, "Brecht & Stalin." Ibid. 50 (May
 1978): 92.

"Capitalism, Socialism, and Democracy." *Commentary* 65 (Apr. 1978): 48-
 50.
 [Reprinted in **Philosophy and Public Policy**, 1980.]

"Civil Discourse and Editorial Responsibility." *Measure* no. 46 (Apr.-May
 1978): 3, 8.

"In Praise of Eduard Bernstein." *Encounter* 50 (June 1978): 76-77.

"Above All, Freedom." Comments on speech by Alexander Solzhenitsyn,
 Harvard Yard, June 1978. *Time* 111 (26 June 1978): 22.

Review of **Challengers to Capitalism: Marx, Lenin, and Mao**, by John G.
 Gurley. *Slavic Review* 37 (June 1978): 307-8.

Review of **My Mind on Trial**, by Eugen Loebel. *Slavic Review* 37 (June
 1978): 323-25.

"Imaginary Enemies, Real Terror." Review of **Delmore Schwartz: The Life
 of an American Poet**, by James Atlas. *American Scholar* 47 (Summer
 1978): 406, 408, 410-12.

"Beyond Freedom Lies Terror." *Business and Society Review* no. 26 (Summer 1978): 15.

"The Case of Alger Hiss." Review of **Perjury: The Hiss-Chambers Case**, by
 Allen Weinstein. *Encounter* 51 (Aug. 1978): 48-55.
 Reply by Eric Jacobs, "Arguments (New & Old) about the Hiss
 Case." Ibid. 52 (Mar. 1979): 80-82.
 Reply by Margaret Stern, "Claims & Counter-Claims." Ibid., 82-83.
 Response by Allen Weinstein, ibid., 83-85.
 Reply by Hook, "A Tale of Mystery--and Detection." Ibid., 85-90.
 [Reprinted in **Philosophy and Public Policy**, 1980.]

Letter to the editor. Comment on Jerome H. Skolnick's review of **Punishing Criminals**, by Ernest van den Haag. *Contemporary Sociology* 7 (Sept.

1978): 528.
    Reply by Skolnick, ibid., 528-30.

Review of **Alienation, Praxis, and Techne in the Thought of Karl Marx**, by Kostas Axelos. *Journal of Economic History* 38 (Sept. 1978): 744-46.

"Home Truths." Review of **Eleanor Marx**, by Yvonne Kapp. *Commentary* 66 (Sept. 1978): 82-86.
[Reprinted in **Philosophy and Public Policy**, 1980.]

"*Bakke*--Where Does It Lead? The Triumph of Racism?" *Freedom at Issue* no. 47 (Sept.-Oct. 1978): 3-6.
    Contribution by Nathaniel R. Jones, "Marshall Points the Way." Ibid., 3-6.
    Rejoinder by Jones, ibid., 7, 12.
    Rejoinder by Hook, ibid.
[Reprinted in **Philosophy and Public Policy**, 1980.]

"Justice for All; Preference for Some?--The Case Against." *Bell Telephone Magazine* 57, no. 5 (Autumn 1978): 24-25, 27.
[Reprinted in **Philosophy and Public Policy**, 1980.]

"Solzhenitsyn and Secular Humanism: A Response." *Humanist* 38 (Nov.-Dec. 1978): 4-6.
    Reply to Tibor R. Machan, "Capitalism's Ethical Imperative: An Answer to Solzhenitsyn's Harvard Commencement Address." Ibid. 38 (July-Aug. 1978): 14-17.

1979

"The Conceptual Structure of Power--An Overview." In **Power: Its Nature, Its Use, and Its Limits**, edited by Donald W. Harward, 3-19. Boston: G. K. Hall and Co., 1979.

"Anti-Semitism in the Academy: Some Pages of the Past." *Midstream* 25 (Jan. 1979): 49-54.

"David Caute's Fable of 'Fear & Terror.'" Review of **The Great Fear: The Anti-Communist Purge under Truman and Eisenhower**, by David Caute. *Encounter* 52 (Jan. 1979): 56-64.

"Social Democracy Means Human Freedom: A Response to the Conservatives." *New America* 16 (Jan. 1979): 6-7, 12.

"Are There Alternatives to Collective Bargaining?" In **Landmarks in Col-

lective Bargaining in Higher Education, edited by Aaron Levenstein, 150-54. Proceedings of the Seventh Annual Conference, April 1979. New York: National Center for the Study of Collective Bargaining in Higher Education, 1979.

"Cosmology and Ethics." Letter to the editor. *New Republic* 180 (5 May 1979): 7.
> Reply to Henry Fairlie, "By Jupiter!" Ibid. 180 (7 Apr. 1979): 18-21.

"Hook *vs.* Wills." Letter to the editor. *Time*, 21 May 1979, 5.
> Reply to R. Z. Sheppard's review of **Confessions of a Conservative**, by Garry Wills. Ibid., 23 Apr. 1979, 86-87.

Letter to the editor. Comment on Andrzej Korbonski's review of **Nothing But Honour: The Story of the Warsaw Uprising**, by J. F. Zawodny. *Russian Review* 38 (July 1979): 412-14.

"The True Meaning of the Pumpkin." *Warbler* 1 (Aug. 1979): 1-3.

"Political Wish-Thinking and the Eurocommunist Myth." Review of **Eurocommunism--Implications for East and West**, by Roy Godson and Stephen Haseler. *Policy Review* 9 (Summer 1979): 143-47.

"Remembering Max Eastman." Review of **The Last Romantic: A Life of Max Eastman**, by William L. O'Neill. *American Scholar* 47 (Summer 1979): 404-5, 408, 410, 412, 414, 416.

"Solzhenitsyn and Western Freedom." *World Literature Today*, Autumn 1979, 573-78.
[Reprinted in **Marxism and Beyond**, 1983.]

"The Weber Case." Letter to the editor by Hook and Miro Todorovich. *Commentary* 68 (Sept. 1979): 21.
> Reply to Carl Cohen, "Justice Debased: The Weber Decision." Ibid., 43, 53.
> Reply by Cohen, ibid., 21.

"Rebuff to Jane Fonda Logical." *Dallas Morning News*, 23 Nov. 1979, 35A.

"Trotsky: The Prophet Who Failed." *New America* 16 (Dec. 1979): 6-7.
> Reply by Otto Nathan, ibid. 18 (Jan.-Feb. 1981): 4.
> Response by Hook, ibid.

1980

Philosophy and Public Policy. Carbondale and Edwardsville: Southern
Illinois University Press, 1980.
 [Reviewed in *America* 142 (31 May 1980): 464-65 (Robert F. Drinan);
 American Spectator 13 (Aug. 1980): 40-41 (Arnold Beichman); *Canadian
 Public Administration* 25 (Fall 1982): 421-22 (Willard A. Mullins);
 Choice 18 (Sept. 1980): 161-62; *Christian Century* 97 (23 Apr. 1980): 476;
 Commentary 70 (Oct. 1980): 74, 76-77 (Werner J. Dannhauser); *Educa-
 tional Studies* 11 (Fall 1980): 315 (Walter P. Krolikowski); *Encounter* 55
 (Nov. 1980): 71-73 (Constantine FitzGibbon); *Ethics* 93 (July 1983): 834
 (Peter G. Brown); *Horizons* 8 (Spring 1981): 191-92 (Joseph W. Devlin);
 Library Journal 105 (15 May 1980): 1169 (Peter Vari); *Modern Age* 25
 (Summer 1981): 308-10 (J. Brooks Colburn); *Modern Schoolman* 60
 (Jan. 1983): 130-31 (Vernon J. Bourke); *Nation* 231 (20 Dec. 1980): 680-
 81 (Philip Green); *National Review* 32 (31 Oct. 1980): 1335-36 (Jeanne
 Wacker Sobran); *New Oxford Review* 48 (Jan.-Feb. 1981): 26-28 (Erazim
 Kohák); *New York Times Book Review*, 30 Nov. 1980, 9 (Nathan Glazer);
 ibid., 8 Feb. 1981, 7, 24-25 (Hilton Kramer); *Perspectives in Religious
 Studies* 8 (Summer 1981): 175, 177-79 (Robert M. Helm); *Philosophical
 Books* 22 (Oct. 1981): 232-34 (Antony Flew); *St. Louis Post-Dispatch*, 30
 Mar. 1980, 4C (Joseph Losos); *Time* 115 (28 Apr. 1980): 92 (Stefan Kan-
 fer); *Wall Street Journal*, 3 Sept. 1980, 26 (Carl Gershman).]

Introduction to **The Middle Works of John Dewey, 1899-1924**, edited by
 Jo Ann Boydston, vol. 9, ix-xxiv. Carbondale and Edwardsville:
 Southern Illinois University Press, 1980.

Preface to **Countdown 1984: A Review of Federal Government "Minority"
 Group Preference in Small Business and Public Works Programs,** by
 James H. Wentzel, iii-iv. Washington, D.C.: National Legal Center for
 the Public Interest, 1980.

"On Western Freedom." In **Solzhenitsyn at Harvard,** edited by Ronald
 Berman, 85-97. Washington, D.C.: Ethics and Public Policy Center,
 1980.
 Comment on Aleksandr I. Solzhenitsyn, "A World Split Apart."
 Ibid., 3-20.

"Liberalism and the Jews: A Symposium." *Commentary* 69 (Jan. 1980): 46-47.

"Memories of John Dewey Days: An Autobiographical Fragment." [St.
 John's] *College* 31 (Jan. 1980): 79-83.

"The Soviet Britannica: An Intellectual Obscenity." *Midstream* 26 (Feb.

1980): 21-22.

"Isaiah Berlin's Enlightenment." Review of **Against the Current**, by Isaiah
Berlin. *Commentary* 69 (May 1980): 61-64.

"The 'Radical' Tilt against Academic Freedom." *Measure* no. 50 (Spring
1980): 1-2.

"Spectral Marxism." Review of **Main Currents of Marxism: Its Rise,
Growth, and Dissolution: The Founders; The Golden Age; The Breakdown**, by Leszek Kolakowski. *American Scholar* 49 (Spring 1980): 250,
252, 254, 256, 258, 260, 262, 267-71.
[Reprinted in **Marxism and Beyond**, 1983.]

"Marx for All Seasons." Review of **Marxism: For and Against**, by Robert
L. Heilbroner. *Commentary* 70 (July 1980): 78-80.
    Reply by Seymour Yellin, "Marx & Marxists." Ibid. 70 (Sept. 1980):
        24.
    Response by Hook, ibid.
[Reprinted in **Marxism and Beyond**, 1983.]

"The Institute for Social Research--Addendum." *Survey* 25 (Summer 1980):
177-78.

"Bertrand Russell's 'Reserve.'" *Midstream* 26 (Aug.-Sept. 1980): 64.
    Reply to Harry Ruja's "Bertrand Russell on the Jews." Ibid. 26
        Feb. 1980): 50-52.
    Response by Ruja, ibid. 26 (Aug.-Sept. 1980): 64.

"Academic Freedom in Jeopardy--Time to Strike the Alarm Bell." *Measure*
no. 53, supp. (Sept. 1980): 1-2.

Review of **The Present Danger**, by Norman Podhoretz. *American Spectator*
13 (Sept. 1980): 32-33.
    Reply by Frank O'Connell, "An Inordinate Fear of Labor? I." Ibid.
        14 (Jan. 1981): 25, 36.
    Reply by Paul Gottfried, "An Inordinate Fear of Labor? II." Ibid.,
        36.
    Rejoinder by Hook, ibid., 36-37.

"Reflections on Tenure and Confidentiality." *Measure* no. 54 (Oct. 1980): 1,
3.
    Reply by Philip Groth, ibid. no. 57 (Summer 1981): 2, 6.
    Rejoinder by Hook, ibid., 2.

"Disremembering the Thirties." Review of **The Dream of the Golden**

Mountain: Remembering the Thirties, by Malcolm Cowley. *American Scholar* 49 (Autumn 1980): 556-60.
[Reprinted in **Marxism and Beyond**, 1983.]

"Righting Marx." *American Spectator* 13 (Oct. 1980): 36.
Reply to Arnold Beichman's review of **Philosophy and Public Policy**. Ibid. 13 (Aug. 1980): 40-41.

"Misread 'Secular Humanist Declaration.'" Letter by Hook and Paul Kurtz. *New York Times*, 7 Nov. 1980, A26.
Reply to Kenneth A. Briggs, "Secular Humanists Attack a Rise in Fundamentalism." Ibid., 15 Oct. 1980, A18.
Reply to Samuel A. Turk, ibid., 25 Oct. 1980, 22.

"Call to Conscience." Letter by Hook et al. on erosion of the United Nations. *New York Times*, 14 Dec. 1980, E7.

"Books for Christmas." *American Spectator* 13 (Dec. 1980): 23.

"The Ground We Stand On: Democratic Humanism." *Free Inquiry* 1 (Winter 1980-81): 8-10.

1981

Introduction to **The Later Works of John Dewey, 1925-1953**, edited by Jo Ann Boydston, vol. 1, vii-xxiii. Carbondale and Edwardsville: Southern Illinois University Press, 1981.

Afterword to **A Life in Two Centuries**, by Bertram D. Wolfe, 714-16. New York: Stein and Day, 1981.

Review of **Marx on the Choice Between Socialism and Communism**, by Stanley Moore. *Russian Review* 40 (Jan. 1981): 55-56.

"A Critique of Conservatism." [Phi Kappa Phi] *National Forum* 61 (Spring 1981): 21-24.

"The Autonomy of Moral Judgment." *Free Inquiry* 1 (Spring 1981): 7.
[Part of "The Secular Humanist Declaration: Pro and Con," ibid., 6-12. See "A Secular Humanist Declaration," ibid. 1 (Winter 1980-81): 3-7.]

"Misrepresentation." *New York Times Book Review*, 12 Apr. 1981, 39.
Reply to Alfred Kazin, ibid., 15 Mar. 1981, 29.

"Jacobo Timerman." Letter to the editor. *New York Times Book Review*, 2

Aug. 1981, 24.
> Reply to Anthony Lewis's review of **Prisoner Without a Name, Cell Without a Number**, by Jacobo Timerman. Ibid., 10 May 1981, 1, 30-32.

"'The Future Danger.'" *Commentary* 72 (Aug. 1981): 4.
> Reply to Norman Podhoretz, "The Future Danger." Ibid. 71 (Apr. 1981): 29-47.

"Popper/Skinner Debate." *Free Inquiry* 1 (Summer 1981): 3.
> Response to letters by Karl Popper and B. F. Skinner on the Secular Humanist Declaration, ibid. 1 (Spring 1981): 3-4.
> Reply by Corliss Lamont, ibid. 1 (Fall 1981): 3.
> Rejoinder to Lamont by Hook, ibid. 2 (Winter 1981-82): 39-40.
> Reply by Dora Black Russell, ibid. 2 (Spring 1982): 5.

"So Schoen War's Frueher Mal in Kalten Krieg." *Die Welt*, 12 Sept. 1981, Geistige Welt section, 1.

"A Million-Dollar Gift's Forbidding Proviso." Letter to the editor. *New York Times*, 10 Oct. 1981, 24.
> Reply to Dudley Clendinen, "Gift to Amherst College Requiring Black Professor Stirs Debate." Ibid., 14 Sept. 1981, 16.
> Comment by Hook, "To the President of Amherst College." *Measure* no. 58 (Fall 1981): 1.

"Human Rights and American Foreign Policy: A Symposium." *Commentary* 72 (Nov. 1981): 40-41.

"The Worldly Ways of John Kenneth Galbraith." Review of **A Life in Our Times**, by John Kenneth Galbraith. *American Spectator* 14 (Oct. 1981): 7-12.
> Response by John Lukacs, "Galbraith Unhooked." Ibid. 15 (Feb. 1982): 29, 40-41.
> Reply by Hook, "Lukacs Hooked." Ibid., 41-44.
> [Reprinted in **Marxism and Beyond**, 1983.]

"Communism and the American Intellectuals from the Thirties to the Eighties." *Free Inquiry* 1 (Fall 1981): 11-15.
> Reply by Lawrence Cranberg, "Is Marx Refutable?" Ibid. 2 (Winter 1981-82): 5, 44.

"Books for Christmas." *American Spectator* 14 (Dec. 1981): 16.

1982

"General Education in a Free Society." In **Freedom, Order, and the University,** edited by James R. Wilburn, 31-41. Malibu, Calif.: Pepperdine University Press, 1982.

"Soviets Won't Honor Freeze." *Stanford Daily*, 23 Apr. 1982, 4.
     Comment by Hook, "Key Omission?" Ibid., 30 Apr. 1982, [n.p.].
     Reply by Joe Walder, "Anti-Soviet Propaganda Falsely Accepted."
          Ibid., 4 May 1982, [n.p.].
     Response by Hook, "Verifying a Nuclear Freeze." Ibid., 13 May
          1982, 4.

"Rights for Potential Crime Victims." *Newsday*, 13 May 1982, 80.

"A Call for the Critical Examination of the Bible and Religion." Statement
     by Hook et al. *Free Inquiry* 2 (Spring 1982): 1, 48.

"Out of the Depths." Review of **The Time of Stalin: Portrait of a Tyranny,**
     by Anton Antonov-Ovseyenko. *American Scholar* 51 (Spring 1982): 291-
     95.
     [Reprinted in **Marxism and Beyond,** 1983.]

"My Running Debate with Einstein." *Commentary* 74 (July 1982): 37-52.
     Replies by Maynard Kniskern and Otto Nathan, ibid. 74 (Nov. 1982):
          16-17.
     Response by Hook, ibid., 17-18.
     Reply by Stephen Siteman, ibid. 74 (Dec. 1982): 76-77.
     Response by Hook, ibid., 77-78.

"A Dissent on Kohrmon." *Brattleboro (Vt.) Reformer*, 4 Aug. 1982, 4.
     Reply to Katherine Kohrmon, ibid., 31 July 1982, 4.

"The First Amendment vs. the Rest of the Constitution." *Denver Post*, 26
     Sept. 1982, 3B.

"An Interview with Sidney Hook at Eighty." *Free Inquiry* 2 (Fall 1982): 4-
     10.
          Comment by Edwin H. Wilson, ibid. 3 (Summer 1983): 3.
          Reply by Hook, ibid., 3-4.
          Editorial comment, ibid., 4.

"The Battle Continues." *Measure* no. 59 (Winter 1982): 1, 3-4, 6.

"A Symposium: The Bishops and the Arms Race." Hook et al. *New York*

Times, 26 Dec. 1982, E3.

"The Soviet Threat to Peace and Freedom." *Washington Times*, 9 Dec. 1982, 15A.

"Living with Deep Truths in a Divided World." *Free Inquiry* 3 (Winter 1982-83): 30-31.

1983

Marxism and Beyond. Totowa, N.J.: Rowman and Littlefield, 1983. [Reviewed in *American Scholar* 52 (Autumn 1983): 558-63 (Lewis S. Feuer); *Best Sellers* 43 (1 Apr. 1983): 30 (James O'Malley); *History Teacher* 20 (Nov. 1986): 126-27 (John W. Long); *Library Journal* 108 (1 Mar. 1983): 502 (Robert C. O'Brien); *Midstream* 29 (Nov. 1983): 51-54 (Lewis S. Feuer); *National Review* 35 (11 Nov. 1983): 1422-23 (Joseph Sobran); *New Leader* 66 (16 May 1983): 7-9 (Irving Louis Horowitz); *New York Times Book Review*, 10 Apr. 1983, 16 (Judith K. Davison); *Publishers Weekly* 223 (21 Jan. 1983): 76; *Studies in Soviet Thought* 28 (Oct. 1984): 245-49 (Maurice A. Finocchiaro); *This World* 5 (Spring-Summer 1983): 149-53 (Mark Lilla); *Village Voice Literary Supplement*, no. 24, Mar. 1984, 1, 10-14 (Paul Berman).]

Foreword to **The Politics of John Dewey**, by Gary Bullert, 3-5. Buffalo, N.Y.: Prometheus Books, 1983.

"Ominous Rumblings in the Academy." *Measure* no. 61 (Mar. 1983): 1, 8.

"Hook: The Test Is Always the Quality, Not Quantity, of Scholarly Works." *Campus Report* (Stanford), 11 May 1983, 11.

"The Morality of Survival in a Nuclear Face-Off: People with Courage to Fight for Freedom Have the Best Chances of Avoiding Misery." *Los Angeles Times*, 11 May 1983, Part II, 5. [Commentary adapted from **Marxism and Beyond**.]

"Edging Towards Disaster?" *Measure* no. 62 (May 1983): 1, 8.

"What Can Be Done?" *Measure* no. 62 (May 1983): 4, 7-8.

"An Open Letter to the U.S. Senate." *Washington Times*, 26 July 1983, 1C.

"Cold Warrior." *Encounter* 61 (July-Aug. 1983): 12-16.

"The Incredible Story of Michael Straight." *Encounter* 61 (Dec. 1983):

68-73.
>Comment by Editors, ibid. 62 (Apr. 1984): 77.
>Response by Straight's lawyer, ibid., 77-78.
>Reply by Hook, ibid., 78.

1984

"Pluralistic Societies at Stake." In **Challenges to the Western Alliance**, edited by Joseph Godson, 177-81. London: Times Books, 1984.

"The Philosopher as a Young Man." Review of **The Collected Papers of Bertrand Russell**, vol. 1, edited by Kenneth Blackwell et al. *New York Times Book Review*, 29 Jan. 1984, 7-8.

"Judging Brecht." *Times Literary Supplement*, 3 Feb. 1984, 111.
>Reply to John Willett, ibid., 13 Jan. 1984, 37.
>Response by Willett, ibid., 17 Feb. 1984, 165.
>Reply by Hook, ibid., 9 Mar. 1984, 247.

"Breaking with the Communists--A Memoir." *Commentary* 77 (Feb. 1984): 47-53.

"New York Intelligentsia." Letter by Hook and Arnold Beichman. *New York Times Book Review*, 25 Mar. 1984, 26.
>Reply to Nathan Glazer, "New York Intellectuals--Up From Revolution." Ibid., 26 Feb. 1984, 1, 34-35.

"Mill on Nonintervention." Letter to the editor. *New York Times*, 25 April 1984, A22.
>Comment on "Moynihan to Quit Senate Panel Post in Dispute on C.I.A." Ibid., 16 Apr. 1984, A1, A8.

"Bertrand Russell: A Portrait from Memory." *Encounter* 62 (Mar. 1984): 9-20.
>Comment by Peter Campbell, ibid. 62 (May 1984): 80.
>Comment by Robert E. L. Faris, ibid. 64 (Feb. 1985): 78.
>[Reprinted in **Out of Step: An Unquiet Life in the 20th Century**, 1987.]

"Memories of the Moscow Trials." *Commentary* 77 (Mar. 1984): 57-63.
>Correction by Hook, ibid. 77 (May 1984): 13.
>Reply by Tom Milstein, ibid. 78 (Aug. 1984): 8.
>Reply by Jeremy Murray-Brown, ibid.
>Response by Hook, ibid., 8-9.

"The Myth of Necessity." Review of **The Reality of Communism**, by

Alexander Zinoviev. *Times Literary Supplement*, 6 Apr. 1984, 365-66.
Reply by Robert Gorham Davis, ibid., 11 May 1984, 523.
Response by Hook, ibid., 27 July 1984, 841.

"Basics We Must Not Forget." *Times* (London), 23 April 1984, 10.

"Humanities, Liberal Democracy Need Not Conflict, Hook Says." Text of
Jefferson lecture on "The Humanities and Defense of the Free Society."
Campus Report (Stanford), 30 May 1984, 17-18.
Comment by Bob Beyers, "Hook Advocates Required Study of Free
Democratic Principles." Ibid., 17.

"'Geniemoral.'" *Midstream* 30 (May 1984): 33-36.

"Looking for America." Letter to the editor. *Harper's*, May 1984, 79.
Response to Philip Berrigan's contribution to "Does America Still
Exist?" Ibid., Mar. 1984, 45-46.

"Education in Defense of a Free Society." *Commentary* 78 (July 1984): 17-
22.
Comment by George Field, ibid. 78 (Oct. 1984): 7-8.
Comments by Joseph R. Aziz, Raymond Garmel, and David Broyles,
ibid. 78 (Nov. 1984): 9-10.
Reply by Hook, ibid., 10-11.

"Sweet Are the Uses of Diversity." Letter to the editor. *Wall Street Journal*,
3 July 1984, 25.

"God and the Professors." *Free Inquiry* 4 (Summer 1984): 18-27.
[Reprinted in **Out of Step: An Unquiet Life in the 20th Century**, 1987.]

"Comment on a Comment." *International Journal of World Peace* 1
(Autumn 1984): 41-44.
Reply to Lloyd Motz's "Comment" on Alexander Shtromas, "To
Fight Communism: Why and How?" [Ibid., 20-33.] Ibid., 33-36.
Rejoinder by Shtromas, ibid., 36-41.

"The Principles and Problems of Academic Freedom: Accountability." *Vital
Speeches of the Day* 50 (1 Sept. 1984): 701-4.

"'Evil Empire' Label Didn't Hurt the Kremlin's Feelings." *New York Times*,
4 Nov. 1984, 24E.
Reply to Editorial, "Mondale for President." Ibid., 28 Oct. 1984,
22E.

"The Use and Abuse of Academic Freedom." *Measure* no. 63 (Nov. 1984):

1-2.

"The Academic Ethic in Abeyance: Recollections of *Walpurgisnacht* at New
York University." *Minerva* 22 (Autumn-Winter 1984): 297-315.

"Questions About a Strange Conversion." *Encounter* 63 (Dec. 1984): 65.
Reply to George Urban, "Portrait of a Dissenter as a Soviet Man: A
Conversation with Alexander Zinoviev." Ibid. 62 (Apr. 1984): 8-24,
and ibid. 62 (May 1984): 30-38.

"The Communist Peace Offensive." *Partisan Review* 51 (1984-85): 692-711.
[Reprinted in **Out of Step: An Unquiet Life in the 20th Century,** 1987]

1985

"Three Intellectual Troubadours." *American Spectator* 18 (Jan. 1985): 18,
20-22.

"All Is Not Fair in News Reporting." *Wall Street Journal,* 21 Feb. 1985, 33.

"English Influence Enlightened India." *Detroit News,* 31 Mar. 1985, 17A.

"Rationalizations for Reverse Discrimination." *New Perspectives* 17 (Winter
1985): 9-11.
Reply by James Kilpatrick, "Do Not Benignly Neglect Injustice." *San
Francisco Chronicle,* 16 Apr. 1985, 40.
Reply by Jeffrey Hart, "The Evil of Reverse Discrimination." *St.
Louis Post-Dispatch,* 14 May 1985, 3B.

"Will Capitalists Destroy Capitalism?" *Detroit News,* 19 May 1985, 15A.

"Encounter with Espionage." *Midstream* 31 (May 1985): 52-55.

"Would It Destroy the World?" Review of **Telling Right from Wrong,** by
Timothy J. Cooney. *New York Times Book Review,* 30 June 1985, 13.

"Hook on the Stockdales." *American Spectator* 18 (June 1985): 7.
Comment on Harry G. Summers, Jr., review of **In Love and War,** by
Jim and Sybil Stockdale. Ibid. 18 (Apr. 1985): 41-44.
Reply by Summers, ibid. 18 (June 1985): 7.

"Unacademic Campus Tactics." *New York Times,* 3 Oct. 1985, A27.

"What's Fair about News Reporting?" *Palo Verde Valley Times,* 18 Oct.
1985, 4.

"The Wrong Way to Remedy Abuses of the Academic Ethic." *Measure* no. 64 (Oct. 1985): 1-2, 5.

"Throw Them in the Melting Pot: Experience Shows Immigrant Children Learn English by Being Taught in English." *St. Louis Post-Dispatch*, 24 Nov. 1985, 3G.

"How Has the United States Met Its Major Challenges Since 1945? A Symposium." *Commentary* 80 (Nov. 1985): 47-50.

"'Class Consciousness' in the Free World." *New America* 22 (Nov.-Dec. 1985): 3.

"Bilingual Ed: Aid or Obstacle?" *Detroit News*, 10 Dec. 1985, 19A.

"Academy of Humanism News. Ernest Nagel (1901-1985): A Naturalistic Humanist." *Free Inquiry* 6 (Winter 1985-86): 27.

"On the Existence of God: Duncan and Hook." Correspondence between Homer Duncan and Hook. *Free Inquiry* 6 (Winter 1985-86): 39-41.

"Pluralistic Humanism." *Free Inquiry* 6 (Winter 1985-86): 19-20.

1986

"A Dictionary? Marxism from A to B." *Encounter* 66 (Jan. 1986): 71-74.
    Comment by Tibor R. Machan, "Hook's Marx." Ibid. 66 (May 1986): 76.
    Reply by Hook, "Sidney Hook's Reply." Ibid.
    Comment by Machan, "Hook's Marx." Ibid. 67 (Dec. 1986): 80.
    Reply by Hook, "Sidney Hook Replies." Ibid.

"Between Democracy and Despotism." *Imprimis* 15 (Feb. 1986): 1-4.

"Burden of Proof Is Put on the Defamed." *New York Times*, 6 May 1986, A30.
    Reply to Stuart Taylor, Jr., "High Court Adds Protection for News Media in Libel Suits." Ibid., 22 Apr. 1986, A1, A14.

"Rediscovering Sin." *New York Times Magazine*, 11 May 1986, 86.
    Response to William F. Buckley, Jr., "Thou Shalt Not." Ibid., 6 Apr. 1986, 34-36.

"Punishing the Innocent Is Unjust Redress." *New York Times*, 7 June 1986, 26.

Response to editorial, "Affirmative (to Most People) Action." Ibid.,
24 May 1986, 24.

"Who Lives Where, and When?" *Measure* no. 65 (July 1986): 1, 5-6.

"Anti-Communism on Campus: Misreading of John Dewey, C. G. Jung, and
Santayana." *Chronicle of Higher Education*, 6 Aug. 1986, 36.
    Comment on Michael D. Yates, "South Africa, Anti-Communism,
       and Value-Free Science." Ibid., 14 May 1986, 84.
    Comment on Robert S. Corrington, letter to the editor. Ibid., 18
       June 1986, 37.
    Response by Corrington, "John Dewey's Social Theory and Univ-
       ersity Policy." Ibid., 1 Oct. 1986, 46.
    Reply by Hook, "Dewey's Opposition to Communism." Ibid., 22 Oct.
       1986, 47-48.

"Communists in the Classroom." *American Spectator* 19 (Aug. 1986): 21-24.

"The New School Germanized?" *New York Times Book Review*, 28 Sept.
1986, 45.
    Reply to Nathan Glazer's review of **New School: A History of the
       New School for Social Research**, by Peter M. Rutkoff and Wil-
       liam B. Scott. Ibid., 31 Aug. 1986, 6-7.
    Reply by Rutkoff and Scott, ibid., 28 Sept. 1986, 45.

"Questions Concerning Student PIRGS." *Measure* no. 66 (Sept. 1986): 1-2,
5-6.

"The Principles and Problems of Academic Freedom." *Contemporary
Education* 58 (Fall 1986): 6-12.

"The New Challenges to Our Schools of Journalism." *Measure* no. 67
(Nov.-Dec. 1986): 1-2, 4, 6.

1987

Out of Step: An Unquiet Life in the 20th Century. New York: Harper and
Row, 1987.
    [Reviewed in *American Scholar* 56 (Autumn 1987): 577-86 (Edward
Shils); *American Spectator* 20 (June 1987): 36-38 (William McGurn);
Booklist 83 (1 Jan. 1987): 668 (Bryce J. Christensen); *Book World*
(Washington Post) 17 (3 May 1987): 5-6 (Nathan Glick); *Boston Sunday
Globe*, 29 Mar. 1987, A11, A13 (Robert Gorham Davis); *Choice* 24
(July-Aug. 1987): 1706 (R. H. Evans); *Christian Science Monitor* 79 (23
Apr. 1987): 21 (Merle Rubin); *Chronicles* 12 (Jan. 1988): 34-35 (Paul

Gottfried); *Commentary* 84 (Aug. 1987): 17-23 (Hilton Kramer); *Congress Monthly* 54 (Sept.-Oct. 1987): 16-18 (Irving Louis Horowitz); *Foreign Affairs* 66 (Fall 1987): 195 (Gaddis Smith); *Fortune* 115 (13 Apr. 1987): 122 (Daniel Seligman); *Forward*, 21 Aug. 1987, 26-27 (Albert Glotzer); *Freeman* 37 (June 1987): 236-38 (John Chamberlain); *Grand Street* 7 (Autumn 1987): 185-94 (John Patrick Diggins); *Humanist* 47 (Sept.-Oct. 1987): 45-46 (John P. Runden); *Insight* (Washington Times) 3 (27 Apr. 1987): 62-63 (Paul Johnson); *International Herald Tribune*, 10 Apr. 1987, 16 (John Gross); *Kirkus* 55 (1 Feb. 1987): 197-98; *Library Journal* 112 (15 Feb. 1987): 142 (Raymond Frey); *Nation* 244 (30 May 1987): 726-30 (Robert Westbrook); *National Review* 39 (14 Aug. 1987): 43-44 (M. E. Bradford); ibid. 39 (11 Sept. 1987): 61-62 (Jeffrey Hart); *New Leader* 70 (23 Mar. 1987): 14-15 (John P. Roche); *New Republic* 196 (4 May 1987): 30-31 (Arthur M. Schlesinger, Jr.); *New York Times*, 31 Mar. 1987, C17 (John Gross); *New York Times Book Review*, 12 Apr. 1987, 14-15 (Dennis H. Wrong); *Policy Review* no. 42 (Fall 1987): 82-84 (Richard Grenier); *Publishers Weekly* 231 (13 Feb. 1987): 85-86; *Reason* 19 (Dec. 1987): 49-51 (Robert Nisbet); *Reference and Research Book News* 2 (Summer 1987): 1; *St. Louis Post-Dispatch*, 24 May 1987, 5C (Joseph Losos); *San Francisco Chronicle/Review*, 11 Oct. 1987, 6 (Marion Fay); *Society* 25 (Nov.-Dec. 1987): 94-97 (Paul Hollander); *Time* 120 (30 Mar. 1987): 72 (Stefan Kanfer); *Wall Street Journal*, 15 Apr. 1987, 32 (Nathan Glazer); *Washington Times*, 6 Apr. 1987 (Paul Johnson).]

Soviet Hypocrisy and Western Gullibility, by Hook, Vladimir Bukovsky, and Paul Hollander. Washington, D.C.: Ethics and Public Policy Center, 1987.

Paradoxes of Freedom. With a new introduction by Hook. Buffalo, N.Y.: Prometheus Books, 1987.

"Pages from the History of the Association." *Proceedings and Addresses of the American Philosophical Association* 60 (Jan. 1987): 511-13.

"In Defense of Voluntary Euthanasia." *New York Times*, 1 Mar. 1987, E25.
> Comment by Norman Podhoretz, "A Subliminal Endorsement of Suicide." *Washington Post*, 11 Mar. 1987, A19.
> Reply by John Lofton to Podhoretz, "Euthanasia's Slippery Slope." *Washington Times*, 1 Apr. 1987, D1.
> Reply by Hook to Podhoretz, "Does Euthanasia Send Us Down a 'Slippery Slope'?" Ibid., 23 Apr. 1987, A15.
> Reply by Hook, "Grant the Terminally Ill a Right to Relief from Suffering." *San Jose Mercury*, 21 Mar. 1987.
> Responses by Felicia Ackerman, Lenore Blumenthal, Eric Kocher, and Isaiah Rackovsky, *New York Times*, 20 Mar. 1987, A30.

Reply to Rackovsky, "Life at Any Price Is a Bargain with Infamy." Ibid., 9 Apr. 1987, A26.

"The Affirmative Action Ruling--and the Imperial Judiciary." *New York Post*, 6 Apr. 1987, 21.

"The Doctrine of Moral Equivalence Fails on the Facts." *Orange County Register* [Santa Ana], 16 Apr. 1987, B15.
[Also published in *New York City Tribune*, 28 Apr. 1987, as "'Moral Equivalence'--A Useless, Outworn Doctrine."]

"Santayana: Humanist Misanthrope." Review of **George Santayana: A Biography,** by John McCormick. *Washington Times Magazine*, 27 Apr. 1987, M1, M4.

"Off on Hook." *New Republic* 196 (25 May 1987): 2.
Reply to Arthur M. Schlesinger, Jr., ibid. 196 (4 May 1987): 30-31.

"A Curious Phenomenon: A Report." *Measure* no. 69 (June 1987): 1, 6.

"Educational Statesmanship or Educational Demagogy?" *Measure* no. 69 (June 1987): 4.

"Hook, Russell, and Atomic War." *American Spectator* 20 (June 1987): 9.
Reply to Tom Bethell, "A Stroll with Sidney Hook." Ibid. 20 (May 1987): 11-13.

"The Communist Peace Offensive." *Freedom at Issue* no. 97 (July-Aug. 1987): 13-18.

"James Burnham: Radical, Teacher, Technician." *National Review* 39 (11 Sept. 1987): 32-33.

"Old Wine in New Bottles." Review of **Thinking Like a Communist: State and Legitimacy in the Soviet Union, China and Cuba,** by Tony Smith. *Asian Wall Street Journal*, 22 Sept. 1987, 8.

"Communists, McCarthy and American Universities." Review of **No Ivory Tower: McCarthyism and the Universities,** by Ellen Schrecker. *Minerva* 25 (Autumn 1987): 331-48.

"Why 'Back to Basics' Isn't Good Enough." Interview by Thomas Main. *American Educator* 11 (Fall 1987): 24-28, 42.

"A Common Moral Universe?" *Free Inquiry* 7 (Fall 1987): 29, 31.
Reply to Yaakov D. Homnick, "Hook Is Mired in Secular Confu-

sion." Ibid., 28-29, 30.

"Philosophy & Faith." *Commentary* 84 (Nov. 1987): 2, 4.
>Reply to Hilton Kramer, "The Importance of Sidney Hook." Ibid. 84 (Aug. 1987): 17-23.
>Comment by Lewis S. Feuer, ibid. 84 (Nov. 1987): 4-6.
>Response by Kramer, ibid., 6.

"How to Blow Your Own Horn Effectively." Review of **Inventing the Truth: The Art and Craft of Memoir**, edited by William Zinsser. *Wall Street Journal*, 23 Nov. 1987, 24.

1988

Introduction to **The Machiavellians: Defenders of Freedom**, by James Burnham. Washington, D.C.: Regnery Gateway, 1988.

"Making the Case Against Socrates." Review of **The Trial of Socrates**, by I. F. Stone. *Wall Street Journal*, 20 Jan. 1988, 24.
>Comment by Kate Regan, "Izzy at 80: Wisdom Through the Ages." *San Francisco Chronicle*, 6 Feb. 1988, C3.
>Reply by Hook, "He Was Praised." Ibid., 29 Feb. 1988, A16.

"Absence of Core List of Texts 'Fatal' to Worthwhile Course." *Campus Report* (Stanford), 20 Jan. 1988, 12-13, 17.

"Emotion and Invective Dominate Western Culture Debate." *Stanford Review*, Jan. 1988.

"The Event-making Man." *World and I* 3 (Feb. 1988): 583-92.

"The Attack on Western Civilization: An Interim Report." *Measure* no. 70 (Feb. 1988): 1-5.

Letter to the editor. *New York Times Book Review*, 6 Mar. 1988, 2.
>Reply to Stephen Schwartz, "Intellectuals and Assassins--Annals of Stalin's Killerati." Ibid., 24 Jan. 1988, 3, 30-32.

"The Uses of Death." Review of **Setting Limits: Medical Goals in an Aging Society,** by Daniel Callahan. *New York Review of Books* 35 (28 Apr. 1988): 22-25.

"Educational Disaster at Stanford University." *Measure* no. 72 (Apr. 1988): 1, 3-8.

"'Cultural Philistine.'" Letter to the editor. *New York Review of Books* 35 (12 May 1988): 61.
>> Reply to M. F. Burnyeat's review of **The Trial of Socrates**, by I. F. Stone. Ibid. 35 (31 Mar. 1988): 12, 14, 16-18.
>> Reply by Burnyeat, ibid. 35 (12 May 1988): 61.
> [See "Making the Case Against Socrates," 20 Jan. 1988.]

"The Color of Culture." *Chronicles* 12 (May 1988): 16-19.
> [See "Absence of Core List of Texts 'Fatal' to Worthwhile Course," 20 Jan. 1988.]

"Intellectual Classes and Institutional Values." *Society* 25 (May-June 1988): 66-69.

Title-Subject Index

Name Index

Title-Subject Index

Name Index

Barbara Levine has been a textual editor at the Center for Dewey Studies, Southern Illinois University at Carbondale, since 1974, having taught English at SIU from 1962 to 1974, and at Niles (Ill.) Township High School from 1960 to 1962. She received her B.S. from the University of Wisconsin in 1959 and her M.A. in English from Northwestern University in 1960. She has served as textual editor of volumes 9 and 13 of *The Middle Works of John Dewey, 1899-1924;* of volumes 1, 7, 10, 13, and the forthcoming volume 17 of *The Later Works of John Dewey, 1925-1953;* and of *The Poems of John Dewey,* all edited by Jo Ann Boydston. She is currently compiling a third edition of the *Checklist of Writings about John Dewey.*